Also by Angelo M. Pellegrini

WASHINGTON: PROFILE OF A STATE
(1967)

WINE AND THE GOOD LIFE (1965)

AMERICANS BY CHOICE (1956)

IMMIGRANT'S RETURN (1951)

THE UNPREJUDICED PALATE (1948)

THE FOOD-LOVER'S GARDEN

THE FOOD-LOVER'S
GARDEN ❦ ❦ ❦ ❦ ❦

Angelo M. Pellegrini

ILLUSTRATED BY GRAMBS MILLER

ALFRED · A · KNOPF / NEW YORK / 1970

THIS IS A BORZOI BOOK

PUBLISHED BY ALFRED A. KNOPF, INC.

Copyright © 1970 by Angelo M. Pellegrini

All rights reserved under International and Pan-American Copyright Conventions.

Published in the United States by Alfred A. Knopf, Inc., New York,

and simultaneously in Canada by Random House of Canada Limited, Toronto.

Distributed by Random House, Inc., New York.

Library of Congress Catalog Card Number: 76–106621

Manufactured in the United States of America

Published April 28, 1970
Second Printing, July 1970

THIS BOOK IS FOR MY EDITOR,

Judith B. Jones

Contents

Why a Kitchen Garden?

Why should one bother to till a cut of the land on which he lives and grow much of what he needs for his daily dinner? The reasons are several, but the most compelling is this: the kitchen garden is an indispensable aid in the attainment of a day-by-day good cuisine. Or put it this way: without a kitchen garden—that plot of land on which one grows herbs, vegetables, and some fruit—it is not possible to produce decent and savory food for the dinner table. This generalization admits no exceptions; it is as sound as the assertion that a stone thrown in the air must return to earth. And since a fine dinner after the day's labor contributes so much to one's well-being, I may state, further, that the kitchen garden is an indispensable aid in the achievement of the Good Life. Are you convinced? Of course! Then you must procure the necessary tools and become a gardener.

In urging this, I assume that you are a normal human being, male or female, young enough to stand on your feet and work with your hands; but most of all I must assume that you are eager to welcome hints on how you can improve your cuisine. And I must also cherish the hope that, should you be rather abstemious, or of that wretched crew who take pride in "eating anything," this little volume may persuade you to join that enlightened company who, as Dr. Johnson put it two hundred years ago, "mind their belly very studiously and very carefully." In other words, I assume that you are one of us; and I therefore urge you with confidence to build yourself a garden and become an expert, happy gardener.

Let us first be clear on what we mean by the word "garden." The dictionary defines it as "a plot of ground devoted to the cultivation of useful or ornamental plants." There is, of course, a distinction between plants that are ornamental and plants that are useful; when I use the word "gardening" my reference is invariably to the cultivation of those plants, such as asparagus, that are used as food; and those, such as rosemary, that are used to make food taste good. In other words, my approach to gardening is fundamentally utilitarian. I cultivate as much of the necessary herbs, vegetables, and fruit as time and place and space will allow, in order to enjoy a fine, even a distinguished, dinner every day.

Fundamentally utilitarian, yes. However, I am not unaware of the aesthetics of gardening. I am easily moved by the beauty in a bed of parsley, a head of cauliflower, a patch of healthy, succulent endive in vigorous growth. Even as the poet's heart leaped up when he beheld a host of golden daffodils, so mine throbs when I behold a row of meticulously cultivated cauliflowers, their compact, snow-white heads set in leafy ruffs of emerald green. So please don't put me down as an insensitive Benthamite. My sense of what is useful does not exclude a sense of what is lovely. I cultivate a garden for its utility, to eat that which I grow, but there is also pleasure in doing it and in beholding the fruit of my labor. When, during the growing season, I go to my garden, as I do nearly every day, and look with pleasure at my bed of parsley, am I moved primarily by its indubitable loveliness? Or is my heart throb occasioned by the thought of how marvelously the minced parsley leaves will enhance the flavor of my omelet? The question is not fair, and I invoke the Fifth. In obedience to my nature I till the soil; I sow and reap the total harvest.

I said that you must build a garden, and "build" is the proper word. Wherever you may live, on whatever plot of land that is your own, you will have to convert a portion of that land into a garden plot. With pick and shovel, rake and hoe and barrow, you may have to dig up a portion of the lawn, level a slope, build retaining walls, wheel out hardpan and rocks and wheel in fine topsoil, or make heavy earth more friable by raking into it sandy soil rich in humus. With tools and with your hands you will give shape to your garden and prepare it to receive the seed. You will build your garden.

There will be joy in the building; there will be joy in contemplating that which you have built; there will be joy in the sowing; there will be joy in following the progress from seed into fruit; there will be joy in the harvest; and there will be the greatest pleasure in eating the fruit of your labor. If you have not known this pleasure, then you have been deprived of much that is good for both the body and the soul! Therefore, decide and act. Don't be a Prufrock wavering in indecision, measuring out your life with a coffee spoon. The shovel is the measure appropriate to a man. Strip to the waist; let the sweat pour down your brow; dig in; put down your roots. And enjoy a manifold harvest.

So, having taken in hand the shovel and the hoe, you have become a dedicated gardener and a member of an ancient and numerous society. The Great Creator built the first garden and created the prototypes of the complete gardener. Man first appears not in an armory or in a count-inghouse but in a garden; and when he had sinned and lost his Eden, he was sent forth to till the ground whence he was taken, and to earn his bread by the sweat of his brow. The Old Testament is so rich in horticultural imagery that one may fairly think of the prophets and psalmists as dedi-cated gardeners: *They that have gathered the corn shall eat it and praise the Lord; and they that have grown the wine shall drink it in the courts of my holiness....*

A glance at the considerable library of garden literature, and it is at once obvious that some of the wisest and best of mankind have delighted in gardens. Horace had his garden and his orchard; Virgil celebrated agricultural pursuits in his *Georgics*. Shakespeare compared competent kings to complete gardeners and well-ordered commonwealths to well-cultivated gardens; and when his Brutus was troubled and could not sleep, Shakespeare sent him to his garden to ponder his dilemma. John Evelyn, the famous diarist, Robert Walpole, the first Earl of Oxford, William Temple, the seventeenth-century statesman, and Sir Francis Bacon are a few among the many illustrious men who have de-lighted in gardens. The Baron Bettino Ricasoli, in the mid-dle of the nineteenth century, withdrew from the turbu-lence of public affairs and settled in Brolio Castle in the Chianti region, where he devoted the rest of his life to agronomy and viticulture. The amiable Londoner Charles Lamb, when he went to live in the country, took pleasure in cultivating a small plot of ground behind his house and "watched with interest the progress toward maturity of his Windsor pears and jargonelles."

But it was Sir Francis Bacon, that probing, empirical, and far-ranging mind, who, having studied gardening as an experimental science, finally defined its total goodness in these words: "God Almighty first planted a garden; and, indeed, it is the purest of human pleasures; it is the greatest refreshment to the spirits of man; without which buildings and palaces are but gross handy-works; and a man shall ever see that, when ages grow to civility and elegance, man comes to build stately sooner than to garden finely: as if gardening were the greater perfection."

I remember that when I was a child less than ten years of age, old enough to spade and to hoe and to put seed into the ground, I marveled at the miracle of seed into fruit, mine as good and lovely as that from seed put into the ground by older hands than mine. And now, several decades later, I still marvel at the same miracle, and at all the good things I can grow for the table on a patch of ground so tiny that, from its center, the wind with me, I can spit to its every boundary. As I work on that handful of earth and find myself so easily, so ingenuously excited by such a commonplace phenomenon as the growth of the soil, I have the most vivid perception of Bacon's meaning when he said of gardening that it is the purest of human pleasures and the greatest refreshment to the spirit. More than once when the well was dry and the mood of Ecclesiastes threatened, I followed Brutus to the garden, where all was sweet fruitfulness and nothing was in vain. And I have often wondered, walking among my growing family of vegetables, whether Lord Bacon and Baron Ricasoli and all the great men who delighted in gardening marveled even as I did as a child, and still do as a man, at the recurring miracle of seed into flower. Is there not something that is just right, simply and sweetly good in tilling the soil, sowing the seed, reaping the harvest?

But let us return to something more tangible. Andrew Borde, physician to his "prepotent Majeste" King Henry VIII, another British gentleman who minded his belly very studiously and very carefully, went on record with this practical observation: "It is a commodious and pleasant thing to a mansion to have an orchard of sundry fruits; but it is more commodious to have a fair garden, replete with herbs of aromatic and redolent savour."

Fair, commodious, pleasant! Utility and ornament! Consider, for a moment, the garden as a "commodious" adjunct to one's "mansion"; note what it means in terms of simple well-being, convenience, and domestic economy. Let us suppose that we are gardeners. We have pork cutlets in the cooler. The dinner hour is nigh and we are hungry. Hunger in a gardener has a way of relating to the garden. How shall we enhance the cutlets? We go to the fair garden, replete with herbs of aromatic and redolent savor. We take of these what we want for an appropriate herb marinade. We lave the cutlets with it, sprinkle them with salt and pepper, and put them in the broiler. We pull the cork on a bottle of red wine and as we sip, the aroma of the broiling cutlets in our nostrils, we count our blessings. Then we sit to supper and know the meaning of simple well-being!

But there is yet more of well-being, much more! During the growing season, the garden is a continuous source of fresh vegetables. Now what, precisely, is a fresh vegetable? Anyone who is in the least aware of what he buys at the supermarket must have been many times disappointed when he searched the vegetable bins: the lettuce was wilted; the carrots looked old and tired; the green beans had the pox. With a shrug of futility he took what was least offensive and hoped for better luck next time. The advantage enjoyed by the gardener is that he is never disappointed; his carrots are always taken directly from the garden to the kitchen. And so are the green beans, taken from the vine *when they are prime for the table and cooked immediately*. A vegetable is not necessarily fresh because it is brought immediately from the garden to the kitchen; it may have lost its freshness before it was harvested. A vegetable is completely fresh when it is taken in its prime and brought directly from the garden to the kitchen. On this subject I shall have much to say in Part Three of this book.

Note now the meaning of Andrew Borde's "commodious" in terms of the practical convenience that a garden provides. When well planned, executed, and maintained, the garden will have in it such basic herbs and vegetables as can be grown in a given region, and these will be at hand throughout the growing season. That in itself is the great convenience: to have in one's own garden whatever vegetables one wants, and to have them at the moment he wants them. But the garden is a convenience in other less spectacular, but no less important, ways. A cook needs a sprig of parsley to execute a recipe. Three steps into the garden and he has it. Or he may need a bay leaf, a leaf of chard, a few leaf ends of celery, a small carrot, to flavor a beef broth. Lacking a garden he would have to buy these ingredients in quantities considerably greater than his need, since vegetables are now sold in bunches or packaged in cellophane. What a convenience, then, to take them fresh from the garden in exactly the amount needed. And, incidentally, what a savings! Or, again, the need for a certain indispensable ingredient may be discovered at the last minute, when kettles are boiling and skillets are simmering. The lamb stew is assembled and cooking. All it wants to round out the flavor is a bit of fresh, minced rosemary. And there is the herb, a few paces from the kitchen door. Very commodious indeed!

Granted, one may say; but does it pay? The economy of a kitchen garden is often questioned by people who have little knowledge of what produce costs and no idea how much can be grown on a small plot of land. Typical of such is a man in our neighborhood I call Uncle Harry for no better reason than that he looks as if he might be Uncle Harry to the world. He is a realtor who owns much land hereabout and walks around a great deal, stopping by property he owns and by land he would like to own and wondering all the while which of the many deals he has plotted is ready for execution. He is a fattish, hearty man of affairs who habitually thinks big. He passed by one day while I was setting out cabbage plants. "What the hell are you doing on this fine day?" he asked. And when I told him he said, "Hell, it don't pay. For a couple of bucks you can buy enough cabbage to fatten a steer. Seed, fertilizer, water, labor—you add all these up and you're losing dough. Get wise. Go play golf." I told him I thought he was right, and that made him very happy. "Hell, yes," he said. "It don't pay."

But Uncle Harry was completely wrong, even about fattening a steer on cabbage. A small kitchen garden, properly managed, will put money in your purse. Keep it in production as long as the weather in your region permits; exploit fully the resources of your land; do all that needs to be done, properly and at the right time; and you will prove Uncle Harry wrong.

Our kitchen garden, which I shall describe in detail in Chapter 3, is rather small, a land area 30 by 50 feet, or 1,500 square feet. Since we live in the relatively mild Pacific Northwest, the growing season for a number of vegetables extends into the winter. The tax on our home, in Seattle, where real estate taxes are relatively low, is about $280 a year. On one sixth of the garden area I grow shallots, garlic, and artichokes. The value of these when harvested, reckoned on current supermarket prices, is nearly the equivalent of the real estate tax on our home. Do you doubt it?

Then let me ask you to inquire at the supermarket what shallots, garlic, and artichokes cost!

Such are the facts. Does the kitchen garden pay? Draw your own conclusions. Then forget dollars and cents. Build yourself a garden and reap a manifold harvest of values money cannot buy.

PART ONE

Of Gardening in General

ONE

The Art and Science
of Gardening

The work is easy and pleasant; the art is simple; the science is elementary. There is no one who has even as little wit as a fool who cannot become a very good gardener. And yet there is the myth of the green thumb. People who cannot distinguish a turnip leaf from a chard too easily persuade themselves that they are not cut out to be gardeners.

Nonsense! A green thumb is a disciplined, diligent, working thumb, and it can be yours as well as mine. The inability to distinguish one growing vegetable from another does not mean that one has no aptitude for gardening; what it usually means is that one has never before had occasion to see the two vegetables and note how they differ.

So it is no cause for wonder that the vast majority of men and women, taken on a tour of a vegetable garden at the peak of the growing season, would fail to identify any but the most common plants. We are an affluent, urban, sophisticated society, and our ruling principle in production is specialization. We live exclusively by what we buy, not by what we produce. And much of the produce we buy is either frozen and hidden in foil or trimmed, washed, and wrapped in cellophane. Only a few of us have had the pleasure of seeing, growing in the sun, the vegetables we eat. And the farther we get from growing that which we eat, the more we tend to think of ourselves as lacking in gardening talent.

And yet that which we no longer do, because the structure of our economy no longer requires us to do it, can easily be done. We no longer make beer or mead or wine; we no longer bake bread; we no longer grow the vegetables we need; we are becoming more and more dependent on the precooked frozen dinner. And we are becoming less happy in our surrender of so much self-reliance. For years now I have seized every opportunity that has come my way as a teacher, writer, and lecturer to drive home the point that making wine, baking bread, growing herbs and vegetables, and cooking fine meals are very simple undertakings; that the achievement of excellence in them is within the competence of everyone; and that the joy of the *vital* work these pursuits entail is unique and unutterable. Put me to the test, and thou shalt see! Begin by building yourself a garden.

I said the work is pleasant, the art simple, the science elementary. Let me begin the proof of these declarations with an account of what happened in our family last season. My daughter, Angela, and her husband, Tom Owens, bought a house. The lot was all in lawn, flowers, and shrubbery. They decided to convert part of it into an herb and vegetable garden. Although Angela had seen me gardening when she lived with us, neither of them had ever done any gardening. Tom had never even seen a hoe or a rake. But they wanted a garden, and after coming to me for advice, they proceeded, working together, to build themselves one. They dug up lawn, removed shrubs, uprooted a patch of ivy, built walls, hauled out rocks, hauled in good soil. They worked diligently and happily, and the garden was built. Into the virgin earth, they sowed the seeds of the herbs and vegetables they desired. Then they rested and awaited the harvest.

I noted their zeal, the joy in their labor, the pride in their simple achievements, their discovery of a new source of pleasure. My disciples had done their work well and I was pleased.

I was also a little amazed at their extraordinary success in growing a certain species of peppers. A seasoned, professional gardener could have done no better. Those large, healthy plants, loaded with fruit, were the particular pride of the new gardeners.

They were not the large, bell-shaped peppers, but a species of the pepper family that I have been unable to identify. The pepper is small, about one third the size of a normal bell pepper, and approximately the same shape. It is mild, but with slight intimations of fire; and is more peppery, less sweet than the bell variety.

We had bought 150 plants from an Italian gardener who had brought the seed from Calabria. The Owenses planted half in their new garden and I planted the other half in mine. I taught them how to proceed; we encountered no difficulties. The plants rooted well and were not attacked by pests. But at the height of the growing season, when the first little peppers began to form, it was obvious that the Owenses' peppers were doing better than mine. The plants were larger and more productive. Beginning gardeners had triumphed over their tutor, a man who had been gardening for forty years! We drank a bottle of champagne to their success.

Shall we conclude from this that Tom and Angela Owens are better gardeners, more skilled than I? Perhaps. However, the perfection of their pepper plants was not due to skill. It was due to an abundance of sun. They did what I taught them to do and they did it well; sun and soil did the rest. The pepper plant requires warm weather, and sun the entire day. The Owenses' house is in a section of the city that is somewhat warmer than View Ridge, where we live, and their vegetable garden is in the sun·the entire day. Ours has the morning and only a little of the afternoon sun. All else being equal, as it was, their pepper plants had to be better than ours. And they were.

I have given you this account of the Owenses' success in growing peppers to persuade you that gardening does not require special talents; that the success of your first venture may well match that of a seasoned gardener. Or surpass it. I want now to add that in gardening one may be casual, sensible, or meticulously scientific. He who is casual fails to do all that needs to be done and leaves something to chance; he who is sensible does well all that is necessary to procure a good crop and does no more; he who is meticulously scientific does everything by the book and he does more than is necessary to attain completely satisfactory results. Needless to say, I advise one to pursue the sensible course.

Gardening entails physical labor, working on the land with a peasant's tools; and there are people who have a rooted aversion to such work. Unless they can purge themselves of such aversion, gardening is not for them. However, for people not thus afflicted, the work entailed in gardening on a small scale, for one's own table, is easy, pleasant, relaxing. It is primitive handwork with the soil, a pleasant and invigorating contrast to the often routine, impersonal, work one must do in the shop, the store, the office, the studio. It is a form of body exercise; it makes one sweat; keeps the muscles toned; promotes the enjoyment of food and drink by stimulating hunger and thirst. To indulge in it for a season is to love it forever.

There is a science and an art of gardening; and neither is difficult. One must learn what to do and how to do it well in order to procure a good harvest. Of the two, the science is more readily achieved than the art. I have seen young men strong and intelligent and willing who were unable, for lack of experience, properly and effectively to thrust a shovel into a mound of dirt. One may learn in a few hours when to spade a patch of land and prepare it for the first spring sowing, but it may require several seasons to learn to manage the spade, the hoe, the rake with ease, grace, and effectiveness; to lay out an attractive garden; to distribute crops to best advantage; to exploit with imagination the resources of land, water, and weather. Nevertheless, the art is simple and the mastery of it is within the competence of anyone who will make the effort.

Having decided to build a garden and to proceed sensibly in the venture, what is the least that one must know?

One should have an elementary understanding of soil, its structure, its management, and a knowledge of soil as it relates to plant life. The beginning gardener must learn how to prepare soil for seed and when to put a given seed or plant into the ground. He must learn the function of weeding and cultivating, spacing and thinning, fertilizing and watering. These are the elements of garden science, and they are easily learned.

Consider the familiar soil; establish a relationship with it; have an eye for its many types. A noted soil scientist has defined soil as "friable material in which, by means of their roots, plants may find a foothold and nourishment, as well as other conditions of growth." The study of soil, its structure and composition, is a complex science; but what the amateur gardener needs to know is fairly simple.

Agricultural soil is a mixture of sand, clay, organic matter, and a variety of micro-organisms. A plant will do well when the proportions of these elements in the soil are such as the plant needs for its finest growth. Soil has texture and structure. *Texture* refers to the feel of a soil in the hand when a bit of it is pressed between the fingers. A sandy, coarse-textured soil crumbles easily in the hand. A fine-textured soil, which is mostly clay, will not crumble; when moistened and pressed between the fingers, it becomes a thin, pasty, gummy smear.

A good soil is a well-structured soil. The tiny particles of which it is composed adhere together in aggregates and clusters; *structure* refers to the forms of such aggregates. Some have irregular and others have plane surfaces. The first results in a soil of granular structure; the other, in one that is called blocky. Of the two, the first is much better for gardening.

Some soils are without structure. One that is nearly pure sand, in which every particle is separate from all others, has no structure; nor does one that is nearly pure clay. The latter is called a massive soil, for the grains of which it is composed are bound together in a formless mass that does not crumble. Hardpan and puddled clay are familiar types of massive soil. Soils without structure, whether composed of sand or clay, are not suitable for agriculture.

A well-structured soil suitable for agriculture may be high or low in acid or alkali; it may be relatively neutral; or it may range somewhere between the extremes of acidity and alkalinity. Some plants require an acid and some an alkaline soil. Most, nearly all, vegetables and herbs require a relatively neutral soil. A soil that is excessively acid or alkaline is generally barren and unproductive. Therefore, a gardener must know the acid and alkaline content of the soil in which he intends to grow his herbs and vegetables. He must know what the soil scientist calls the "*p*H factor" of his soil.

The *p*H factor is a symbol used to express the acidity or alkalinity of a soil. Number 7 on the *p*H scale represents the neutral point, where the soil is neither acid nor alkaline. The numbers from *p*H 7 to *p*H 12 represent increasing degrees of alkalinity; from *p*H 7 to *p*H 0, increasing degrees of acidity. Soils with a *p*H factor of 8 or above are too alkaline for plant growth; and those with a *p*H factor of 4 or below are too acid. Soils that are near the two extremes can be corrected. The ones that are excessively alkaline can be made neutral, or nearly so, by the addition of a peat moss high in acid; the acid soils can be rectified by the addition of ground limestone.

These are the elementary elements of soil science; it is wise for all sensible gardeners to know them. The man who is born to the soil, even the illiterate peasant, through long intimacy with the soil as it relates to plant life, knows them without knowing their terminology. He speaks of "heavy" and "light," "sweet" and "sour" soils. The words "heavy" and "light" refer to texture and structure rather than to weight. A clay soil, fine-textured and with little or no structure, *looks* heavy; it resists the pull of the plow and the thrust of the shovel. A sandy soil, granular and loose, coarse-textured and well structured, *looks* light; it has a minimum resistance to the farmer's tools. And it is better suited for agriculture.

Farmers and gardeners who have no sophistication but a great deal of empirical experience with the soil by which they live have a *sense* of the soil; they know it by its appearance, its feel in the hand, its odor. And when they speak of it as being sweet or sour they are describing, metaphorically, a soil that does or does not respond to their needs. I have seen a farmer hold a handful of dirt caress-ingly and pronounce it sweet with a smile of profound satisfaction. And without having read a book they know how to subdue a stubborn soil to their requirements.

That handful of dirt that brought a smile to the farmer's face was just the right combination of sand, clay, and humus. Sand alone has no structure; it is too loose and will not hold water. Clay alone, which is decomposed rock, is structureless. When wet, it is a gummy mass; when dry, it may be as hard as cement, impervious to air and water. Humus is decomposed vegetable and animal matter. It alone is generally too acid; and it retains so much water that most plants will not grow in it.

However, each of these types of soil, inadequate in itself for agriculture, is indispensable in the formation of soil such as will move a farmer to metaphor and affection. When the three are structured together in proper proportions, he will refer to the soil as light and sweet. The scientist will say that it has a granular structure and that on the pH scale it is nearly neutral. It reveals to the farmer's eye and hand what the expert discovers more accurately in a laboratory analysis: that it is composed of sand, clay, and humus in the right proportions.

Such a soil as this, light and sweet, is nearly ideal for a vegetable garden, for almost all vegetables flourish in a neutral, well-drained soil. So when you build your garden, remember to locate it where it will have at least six hours of the day's sun and make sure that your soil is such as we have described.

Given adequate sun and adequate soil, the next requirement for plant life is a constant supply of plant nutrients. The four principal ones, besides air and water, are nitrogen, phosphorus, potassium, and lime. These must be present in the soil at all times and in proper balance. For the growth of herbs and vegetables, there is no need to lime soil that is nearly neutral. The other three nutrients should be in the soil in these proportions: 5 percent nitrogen, 10 percent phosphorus, and 5 percent potassium. A certain amount of these, perhaps enough of each, will be present in the soil components, particularly in the decomposed organic material. If there is a deficiency, you must supply it, either in the form of manure or a commercial fertilizer mixed according to the 5:10:5 formula. The manufacturer will tell you how to use it.

And that concludes the account of what a sensible gardener ought to know about soil science. He is now ready to build his garden. How shall he proceed? I suggested that his approach may be sensible or meticulously scientific. Let me now explain what I mean. Of the soil that is in his garden, he must have only such knowledge as relates directly to the herbs and vegetables he proposes to grow. He needs no more than that. Now, if he is meticulously scientific, he will begin with a thorough analysis of his soil. He will test it in the laboratory for acidity and alkalinity; he will test it to determine its plant-food deficiencies; he will procure a chart on which are indicated the pH soil requirements of every herb and vegetable he intends to grow; then he will make sure that every plant is grown in its proper pH range.

He may conduct these tests himself; or he may send soil samples to the nearest Agricultural Extension Service station. If he sets up his own laboratory, he will procure a soil test kit, consult the local county agent, enlist the aid of the U.S. Department of Agriculture, and—who knows?—gradually build, along with his garden, a soil-science library. More power to him! And may he enjoy the attempt to be a perfectionist!

However, the results he will achieve from being so meticulous will not be appreciably superior to those attained by one who merely proceeds sensibly. His cabbage will not be so superior as to justify all the care that went into its production. So I urge the gardener to avoid being casual, to proceed with good sense, there being no need to be meticulously scientific. Here is what I mean:

I write on the assumption that, wherever you may live, the soil in your proposed garden, if it can be spaded when dry, will be more or less productive. That is a fairly safe assumption. Soils so acid or so alkaline that they will not sustain plant life are not likely to be found in places where people have established cities and towns. What you are most likely to find, if your soil is not the ideal type or nearly so, is that it is too heavy, too clayey, or too sandy. In this case, a three-inch layer of barnyard manure spaded into the ground will do much, not only to correct the soil, but to supply it with the necessary plant nutrients. I have used a great deal of barnyard manure; I have never had it analyzed to determine whether it contained the necessary nutrients in proper balance, but I have often marveled at the quality of my crops. And that is all I need to know about manure: the soil it enriches produces excellent vegetables.

If your soil is *excessively* sandy, if it *looks* almost like sand, and if water poured on it disappears instantly, then you must spade into it a great deal of peat moss or humus, in addition to some manure. If, on the other hand, the soil is so clayey, so massive that when dry it resists the thrust of a sharp spade, then you have what is called hardpan. You must either take it up bit by bit with a heavy pick, grind it or crush it with whatever means you can devise, mix it with sand and humus, and spread it once more. If your garden is of any size, say a thousand square feet or so, the undertaking will be heroic. Art thou heroic? If not, be sensible. Break up the hardpan; haul it away; and haul in the neccessary topsoil to the depth of a foot.

Your soil, however, is not likely to be pure sand or pure clay; if it isn't a fairly good combination of the two, it may be a little more of the one than of the other. If so, it can be easily rectified by the addition of either sand or humus. The additive, together with manure, where this best of all plant nutrients can be procured, should be spread over the proposed garden area; and then you may proceed with the spading.

In spading or plowing, the sod must be turned upside down because the organic matter on the surface, grass and weeds and leaves or whatever, must be incorporated into the lower soil where the roots of the crops may get at it when it is decomposed. By burying the surface filth in which they thrive, spading destroys many vicious insects. Plant roots need air; so do the many useful micro-organisms that are a vital part of all productive soil. Air is also needed for the biochemical reactions necessary to make nutrients available to plant roots. Spading or plowing permits air to enter into the soil for the performance of all these useful functions.

As we noted above, the gardener spades in order to incorporate into the subsoil whatever organic material, whether vegetation, humus, manure, or combination of these, is on the surface. The decomposed organic matter should be well distributed throughout the soil, from the top to whatever depth the roots of vegetables may penetrate; this is generally no more than a spade's length. To achieve this distribution, the sod must be turned and laid in the trench at an angle of about forty-five degrees rather than directly upside down. This can be most effectively done if the spade is thrust into the sod at about that angle, so that the cut of the sod is wide at the top and tapers sharply toward the bottom. If the thrust of the spade is straight down, and the sod is turned and laid in the trench directly upside down, the organic matter will be buried along one horizontal plane

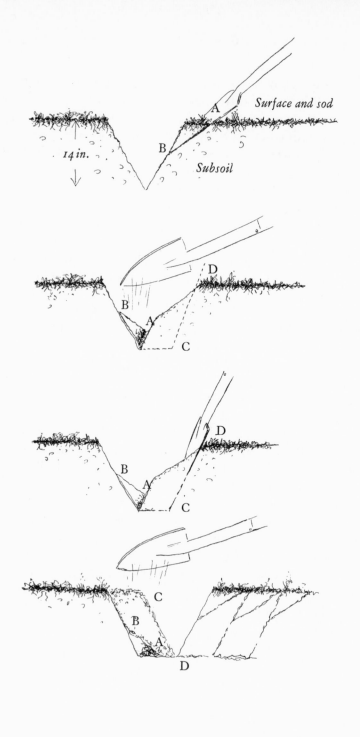

Surface and sod

14 in.

Subsoil

near the bottom of the trench and the plant nutrients in it will be available only to deep-rooted plants.

The beginning gardener may have some difficulty in turning the sod in this way; for there is an art of spading, if one may use that word rather loosely. There is a way of managing the spade with ease and effectiveness. There is an art of hoeing, too, and raking and cultivating, of putting seeds and plants into the ground. And the art, as all other arts, cannot be taught. Each gardener must learn it through experience. In spading a given area, the surface of which is in grass or overspread with humus and manure, one wants to achieve not only a turning of the sod as described above, but also a fairly even and level distribution of the exposed subsoil. The experienced gardener will do this with ease, and his spaded area will please the eye. The unskilled gardener is likely to leave rises and depressions and portions of the organic material exposed. To avoid this he must proceed with care. When he has thrust the spade into the ground and laid down the sod at the proper angle, he must then go straight down with the next thrust into the exposed subsoil and place that on top of the turned sod. As he proceeds he must keep an eye on the spaded ground he leaves behind. Where organic material is exposed, he must cover it; where there are high and low spots, he must redistribute the soil to achieve a level terrain.

The spading must be done when the soil is relatively dry, and if possible, the weather fair. Once the area has been spaded, it should be raked thoroughly. The purpose of raking is to remove rocks and other alien matter from the soil, break up the clods, pulverize the soil as much as possible, and improve the level of the terrain. This is done with the rake drawn in easy back-and-forth movements over the spaded surface, alternately with the tool's prongs and its straight edge to the soil.

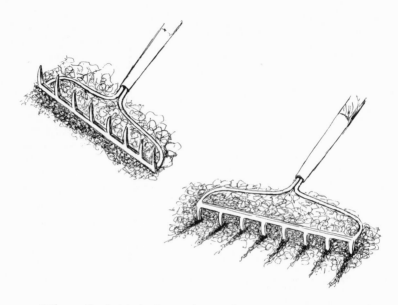

When all of this is done, the gardener is ready to put seed and plant into the ground, each at the proper time. There are different ways of putting seeds into the ground. Before farming was mechanized, the farmer broadcast his grain seed on the land he had prepared for spring sowing. With a bag of seed slung from his shoulder, he walked across his acres flinging fistfuls of seed in a wide arc to the right and to the left. Up and down his land he walked, the pace steady, the fling of the arm strong and graceful, knowing precisely the reach of his fling, until he had covered his acres with seed. These lodged in the tiny crevices on the tilled land, were further embedded in it when the rains came, and germination proceeded apace.

The farmer no longer broadcasts his seed; sowing is now done by machine. But the home gardener, tilling only a tiny plot of land for the love of food, must proceed in the ancient manner. He must put his seed into the ground with his bare hands. He should plan carefully where in the garden each herb and vegetable is to be grown, keeping in mind the size and shape and color of each plant at maturity. Once he has planned his garden, he must decide whether he wants to grow the plants in rows or in rectangular plots.

If he chooses the latter method, each plot should be narrow enough so that its center may be reached, for weeding, thinning, harvesting, from either side; and the plots should be so spaced that he may walk with ease between any two of them. When the plot is laid out, its boundaries set, and the soil properly raked, the gardener may then pretend he is in the nineteenth century and broadcast his seed, whistling with that special merriment that animated the farmer when he thought upon the reaping as he did his sowing. Remembering, however, that his plot is tiny, the gardener must broadcast with restraint, for if he lets fly with all his pent-up energy he will surely fling the seed on his neighbor's lawn. When the seeds are scattered over the entire plot, a gentle tapping of the area with the prongs of the rake will bed them down. Not a *raking* with the rake, but a very light tapping, so that the tines of the tool barely enter the ground, is all that is needed to get the seeds into the soil. Water and sun will do the rest.

There are some vegetables that may be grown to advantage in plots such as I have described. However, I would advise the gardener to plant in rows rather than in plots, especially where the total garden area is small and every square foot of it must be productive. Rows are more easily managed and kept in trim, and waste of space is reduced to a minimum.

The vegetable rows should be straight and evenly spaced, both for the sake of appearance and greater ease in walking between them for weeding and cultivating. To achieve straight and symmetrical planting, even experienced gardeners use a yardstick and guideline, the latter stretched between stakes driven firmly into the ground at opposite ends of the row. Once the row has been situated, the furrow or seed bed is made by drawing the tip of a trowel along the guideline.

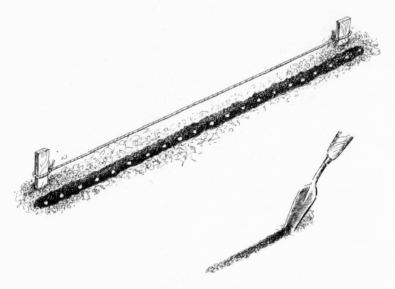

How deep a furrow? Since all vegetable seeds are small, and most of them, such as the seeds of lettuce, carrot, cabbage, very small, the furrow need not be deeper than about an inch. When the furrow is traced, the seeds are deposited in it and covered with about a quarter-inch layer of sand or fine, screened soil; then they are firmed into the ground by gentle tapping with the back of the shovel or hoe. Water and sun will do the rest.

In laying out the rows and putting seeds or young plants into the ground, one must bear in mind that a plant needs space both above and below the ground. Like human beings, plants do not thrive in shadow. This is an elementary horticultural principle, and the beginning gardener seems to have difficulty abiding by it. He tends to put too many plants in a given space. And this is understandable, since seedlings are very small and so many seeds are nearly microscopic.

I myself, after so many years of experience in horticulture, must be constantly on guard against the temptation to put four plants where there is adequate space for only three. Twenty years ago I put into the ground a pine seedling that was eighteen inches long and no bigger in circumference than one's finger. Ten feet away from it I planted a mountain ash that was only slightly larger than the pine. The distance between them seemed more than adequate. The pine today is a foot and a half in diameter; it is about forty feet high; and the horizontal spread of its branches is twenty-five feet. The ash is nearly as large. Where the two trees front each other, the branches of the one intrude upon the other and they are all stunted. When now I am ready to put little cabbage plants into the ground, I glance at that gross error before I space the second from the first. Give me a few more seasons and the spacing will be just right.

To avoid crowding, then, and to secure adequate spacing between plants, one must keep in mind the dimensions of any given plant at maturity. A lettuce seed, for example, no bigger than the eye of a needle, has latent in it a lettuce plant that will measure about a foot and a half from leaf tip to leaf tip at maturity. And one must remember, also, that when seeds are bought from a reliable dealer the percentage of germination is very high.

So to avoid waste of seeds and much laborious thinning when the seeds have grown into little plants, the gardener must proceed slowly and patiently when putting seeds into the furrow. One or two seeds dropped into the furrow an inch apart will yield enough seedlings; this is true of nearly every vegetable. When the little plants are about an inch long, he should proceed with the thinning, that is, remove as many plants as must be taken up in order to provide adequate space between them.

Each plant needs a certain space for its roots in the ground and for its leaves and branches above the ground. Leaves draw nutrients from the air as roots draw them from the ground. The spread of a plant's leaves and the range of its roots are the measure of the space it requires, below and above the ground, whence to draw its sustenance.

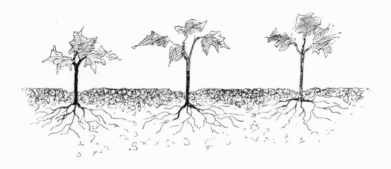

Therefore, if a plant is to do its best, no other plant must be allowed to intrude into its ground and air space. The ideal distance, then, between plants is such that at maturity the leaf tips of one will not touch those of another; and where the spacing is adequate above ground, it is certain to be adequate below.

Related to proper spacing in horticulture are weeding and cultivating. In cultivation, one scratches the surface soil around plants and breaks the crust that forms, so that both air and water can get to the roots. In weeding, one removes all vegetation from a row of vegetables that does not belong there; this is done so that the vegetable itself may have all the soil's fertility. Thus, both weeding and cultivating are processes designed to aid the plant in taking full advantage of all the nutrients in its little world, the space that is adequate to the range of its roots and the spread of its leaves.

Of course, the several horticultural processes relate one to the other, and all of them have as their objective the growing of the best vegetables possible in a given place. A few years ago when I was doing field research for a profile of the state of Washington, I lived with cattlemen, wheat growers, timber men, and orchardists in order to learn from them what was being done in plant and animal husbandry in my state at a time when there seemed to be no limit to miraculous achievements in science. What I concluded after I had completed my field research was that cattlemen and timber men, orchardists and wheat men were all amateur ecologists. They made use of knowledge gained in the laboratory in their efforts to create that total environment in which plants and animals would realize their highest potential. In ways more or less similar, they all spaded and fertilized and raked and weeded and cultivated and spaced so that nature, thus aided, might give them the best steer, the best tree, the best fruit, the best wheat, with the least expenditure of money and energy.

As gardeners driven by the love of food, we are of that fraternity. In the plot of land we have, we want to grow a sound, solid, lovely head of cauliflower, the best quality possible. So we do all that needs to be done to aid nature in creating the environment the cauliflower needs for its best growth. And toward that end we work merrily, since we are working for the pleasures of the table and not for profit. The labor itself—tilling the soil with the peasant's tools; learning to master the use of the spade, the hoe, the rake; converting a cut of land into a productive plot—is a joy and its own reward. It is work in the sun, undertaken not in need but in pleasure; it puts muscles to work, gives edge to the appetite, stimulates thirst. It is work that prepares one for the fullest enjoyment of the pleasure of the table, especially on those many occasions when there is something on the dinner menu that we have grown on our own land.

Nor is the work difficult. The tools are light. We set our own pace. We may, whenever we feel the need of it, rest on the shovel, glance at the sky, follow birds in flight or listen to their song, and ponder in silence the tremendous importance of such tremendous trifles as building a little garden for the joy of building and the love of food.

On Planning the Garden

A little garden! How big is a little garden? Let us suppose that you have no experience whatever in gardening and you have decided to build a garden so that you may grow your own herbs and vegetables. There are six in your family. Your house stands on a lot of ordinary size. How much of it shall you put to the plow?

The answer to this question will depend on the answer to other questions: What proportion of the herbs and vegetables you normally use do you propose to grow? How much of your leisure time are you willing to devote to gardening? If you intend to grow only a few of the vegetables your family normally uses, which ones do you have in mind? Let me explore the answers to these questions, then in the next chapter describe my own garden in some detail so that you may have a tangible guide, a starting point in planning your own.

You will need a garden of considerable size if you intend to grow all, or nearly all, the vegetables a family of six normally consumes day by day. Potatoes, peas, beans, corn, beets, cabbage, cauliflower, broccoli, carrots, lettuce: Shall we agree, for convenience, that these ten are the vegetables Americans eat more or less regularly the year round? Add or subtract a few, or substitute others for some of those listed, and the result will be the same. What we want to determine is the land area necessary to grow them.

Vegetable plants differ in size and therefore in the space requirement for each plant. They differ also in the time they require to mature. Lettuce is ready for the table in six weeks; pole beans require about three months; spinach may be harvested seven weeks after the seed is put into the ground. The seed package will indicate when the vegetable is to be planted, as well as its soil, space, and time requirements.

Given all these facts, one may easily compute on paper the land area one will need for growing any given number of vegetables. Let us consider potatoes as an example. They should be spaced 1½ feet apart in rows 3 feet apart. The yield for each plant will average about six potatoes of normal size. Therefore, in a row 30 feet long there will be twenty plants and the yield will be 120 potatoes. To produce 600 potatoes, in rows 30 feet long and 3 feet apart, one must plant five rows, or a total land area of 450 square feet. If we now assume that a family of six will normally consume three potatoes a day, a patch of land 15 by 30 feet will yield to that family enough potatoes for 200 days, about seven months. Do you have so much land available that you can easily devote that large a section of it to seven months' supply of potatoes? The potato requires about five months to mature; that means that land planted to potatoes will be in use from May through September.

If, for whatever reason, you *must* grow all the potatoes your family consumes in a year, you will need about 600 square feet of land, a plot 30 by 20 feet. Now supposing you also want to grow cabbages, broccoli, cauliflower, and Brussels sprouts, twenty of each. These plants are all spaced about 1½ feet apart in rows 1½ feet apart. If you set them out in 30-foot rows, twenty plants to a row, you will need four rows, or about 180 square feet. Add this to the 600 square feet reserved for potatoes, and your total land requirement for these five of the ten vegetables is nearly 800 square feet, a plot 20 by 40 feet. How big a little garden do you want?

Vegetables differ also in their total yield and in the value of that yield. This fact, too, ought to be kept in mind in planning the most advantageous use of the land available for the garden. On one square yard of land, for exmple, one may grow considerably more green beans than peas, reckoned in weight of the edible portion. If we figure about sixteen vines of beans or peas to the square yard, and that is about correct, the yield of the bean vines will be much more than that of the pea. A well-nourished bean vine of the pole variety will grow twice the height of the pea vine and will produce clusters of green beans all the way and for several weeks; so it will produce more pods than the pea. Furthermore, peas are shelled and the pod is discarded, whereas one eats the entire pod of the green bean. Six full-grown pods of the Kentucky Wonder or Oregon Giant variety are enough for a serving, but one would need about five times that number of pods for a serving of green peas.

Thus, once again, if you have limited space, remember these facts when deciding how much you want to use for each of these legumes; and if you have space for only one, you must decide which one to grow. Study carefully the seed catalogs and become familiar with the yield of each vegetable plant and its space requirement. On a strip of land eighteen inches by forty feet, you can grow enough beets or carrots for a family of six for at least nine months. If you do not have space for both, which shall it be? Or shall you divide the available space between them?

The value of the yield of a vegetable plant should be considered in deciding which of two vegetables will be grown where space limitation compels a choice. On a patch of land fifteen feet by thirty, with a little crowding, one may grow seventy-five artichoke plants. The total yield, at current prices, will have a value of well over $100. Shall one plant potatoes on that land or artichokes? On a strip of land eighteen inches by forty feet one may grow two rows of shallots. The value of the total yield, at current prices, will be well over $50. Shall one plant carrots or shallots on that strip?

In planning the size of the garden, then, you must decide which of the several vegetables you want to grow, and you may want to consider the relative values of the various yields. There is also another factor: in regions where the climate makes it possible, one may grow on the same plot of land a crop of early and one of late vegetables. By the end of June, in regions such as the West and South, peas and the first plantings of certain other vegetables, such as lettuce, radishes, and spinach, are harvested. On the land thus released one may grow leeks, savoy cabbages, kale, endive, and other hardy vegetables that mature in the late fall and early winter. Where the climate makes such successive plantings possible, a garden area of 1,000 square feet becomes, in actual production, considerably larger; and if wisely used, it may very well be large enough for the average family.

Finally, how much time do you intend to devote to gardening? I said in the preceding chapter that the work is easy, pleasant, relaxing. And so it is. But a garden may also become a worry and a burden. Whether it becomes a joy or a creeping drudgery will depend on how wisely you planned its undertaking. He plans wisely who lays out a garden he will be able to manage with ease. One who is relatively young and in good health can do considerable work after the daily employment and on weekends; but he may also want to engage in sports and go on weekend excursions. A garden managed with ease will be of such size that its cultivation will not unduly interfere with relaxing activities of a sort other than gardening. If one is willing to devote all his leisure time to gardening, he may plan accordingly, but even so, he must avoid undertaking more than he can do.

He who, wisely, plans to blend his garden work with other activities must also bear in mind that garden work is seasonal; that certain operations must be performed in a limited time; and that much of it must be done in spring and summer when the weather may tempt him to other pursuits. Spading the land, preparing the soil for sowing and planting, laying out the various beds: these operations must be done at the proper time. In order to do them properly and on time, the gardener might have to forgo a fishing trip or a round of golf.

Remember, then, all that I have detailed above, ye who would join me in the joy of growing food for your table. Plan with care before you put plow to your lawn and bulldozer to your shrubbery. Plan with permanence in mind. Do your paper work with care. If your plot of land is now completely landscaped, building a garden will be in the nature of a remodeling job. Do it in such a way that you will be completely happy with the results. If your land is not landscaped, or you are building a new home, perhaps your first, the laying out of your garden will entail less work but no less planning. In either case bear in mind the following:

The kitchen garden should be located in a sunny, well-drained area away from trees and shrubs. Herbs and vegetables require sun at least six hours a day, and though they require a normal amount of moisture, they do not thrive in sodden soil. The ideal site is a gently sloping terrain with a southern exposure. Neither is strictly necessary if soil drainage and sun exposure are adequate. The roots of trees and shrubs range outward from the trunk to a circumference that is roughly coextensive with the spread of their branches. Within that area they consume so much of the soil's fertility that not even grass will grow well in it. Therefore, trees must come down, or the garden plot must be located an appropriate distance from them.

In planning where the various herbs and vegetables are to be placed in the garden plot, remember that some are annuals and others perennials. The latter, such as asparagus, artichokes, rosemary, and sage, are permanent plantings, so they should be planted along one or more of the edges of the plot, where their presence will not hinder the tilling of the soil for the annuals. Some vegetable plants, such as corn and pole beans, grow to a considerable height; these should be located where they will not unduly shade the lower plants. The best arrangement is to group the tall-growing plants at one end of the garden plot, and in rows that run from east to west to correspond with the movement of the sun; for if they are placed athwart the sun's trajectory, the low plants set on either side of the rows of tall-growing ones will be in the shade part of the day. And the shading of one plant by another must be avoided, for no amount of moisture, fertilizer, or skilled loving care will compensate for the lack of sun.

Remember this basic fundamental in all gardening. And remember, also, to rotate the crops. Crop rotation is the means whereby one avoids planting the same vegetable in the same spot in successive seasons. Thus cabbages might be planted where celery was grown the season before. The reason for the rotation is this: Generally speaking, all vegetables will do well enough in a light soil that has been treated with a balanced fertilizer mixed according to the

5:10:5 formula explained in the preceding chapter, and applied to the soil at the rate of ten pounds for every 500 square feet. However, each plant takes from the soil a quantity of nutrients, which differs with each type of plant. Furthermore, some plants, such as the various legumes, about which I shall write in a later chapter, give to the soil as well as take from it. Thus by rotating the crops in the garden, one will keep its fertility in balance.

In planning rotation, bear in mind that some vegetables are planted early and harvested early while others are planted late and harvested late. Insofar as possible all the vegetables in the former category should be grouped together so that when they are harvested the area they occupied may be easily tilled and prepared for the cultivation of the later ones. In regions where the weather makes possible several sowings of the same crops, such as lettuce, radishes, spinach, turnips, during a single growing season, their rotation, especially where space is limited, will require careful planning.

And now a final word about protecting that which you have so carefully built. When your plot of ground is in full production, you may note that the neighbor's children play hide-and-seek in your bean rows, and their dogs mistake your cabbages for fire hydrants. What then? The answer is a fence that can be neither scaled nor penetrated. Such a barrier will also keep out rabbits, if these should happen to be a pest in your region. But it will not afford protection against rodents of various kinds. If these invade your little Eden, you must kill without mercy. If you are not skilled in such warfare, the federal government will gladly teach you. Write to the U.S. Department of the Interior, Fish and Wildlife Service, Washington, D.C., and ask for their various publications on how to wage deadly warfare on moles, mice, rabbits, rats, and woodchucks.

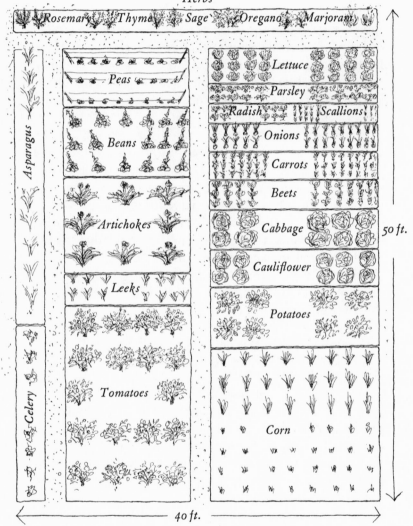

Herbs

Rosemary Thyme Sage Oregano Marjoram

Asparagus

Peas

Beans

Artichokes

Leeks

Tomatoes

Celery

Lettuce

Parsley

Radish Scallions

Onions

Carrots

Beets

Cabbage

Cauliflower

Potatoes

Corn

50 ft.

40 ft.

An Inventory of My Garden

And now will you step into my garden? A survey of it and an inventory of what I grow there may help you in planning your own. Its dimensions are 30 by 50 feet, a land area of 1,500 square feet. Is it a big or a little garden? Well, "big" and "little" are relative terms. So let us simply say that it's bigger than a windowbox and smaller than a farm! It is very productive and more than adequate for the herb and vegetable requirements of a family of five robust appetites. And I built it, quite literally.

Let me describe in some detail how I built it, the labor that went into putting it together, so that you may not be discouraged should the building of your garden present physical obstacles that seem insuperable. For nothing must relax the resolution of a man who is determined to improve his cuisine by growing his own herbs and vegetables. You will note that my garden is somewhat in the nature of a hillside terrace. The lot on which our home is built sloped rather sharply from west to east. Its length, west to east, is 125 feet; its width, 53 feet. I wanted level ground, so I built retaining walls of concrete and reduced the slope to three levels. The first and highest level, at the west end, is 20 feet long and planted to indigenous trees and shrubs. The next level, 3 feet lower, is 70 feet long. On that level are the house, a large patio, a tiny patch of lawn, and extensive flowerbeds. The third level, the east end of the lot, is 4 feet lower and 30 feet long. That is our vegetable and herb garden. Since the lot is 53 feet wide, the land area of the kitchen garden is, roughly, 1,500 square feet.

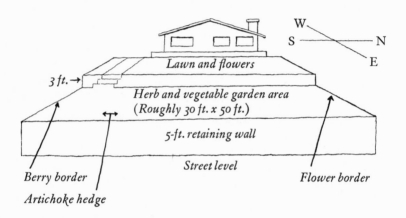

Now if one remembers what I said in the preceding chapter regarding the proper location of the garden, the site of mine would seem to be nearly ideal. The walls that retain it along the northern and southern boundaries rise four feet from street level; the one along the eastern boundary rises six feet. The top of each is flush with the land surface. So the garden area is elevated and therefore well drained. It has also a very slight slope from west to east, determined by the general slope of the terrain. And, as it has both an eastern and a southern exposure, the sunlight is more than adequate.

From the kitchen door to the four steps descending into the garden there is a brick wall flanked by flowerbeds, making the passage from kitchen to garden very pleasant.

I built all the walls myself without aid of man or machine. It was the heaviest kind of common labor, for merely to look at cement makes one's bones ache. But, as I said, nothing must relax . . . And nothing did! And when the walls were built, I built the garden. With pick and shovel and wheelbarrow I put it together. The land I had bought proved to be a mass of pure clay, known among ditchdiggers as hardpan. No shovel could penetrate it when dry, it was so hard. Excellent ground on which to plant a house, but unfit for gardening. The problem was this: either I had to dig up the hardpan, haul some of it away, pulverize the rest and mix it with sandy soil and humus; or raise the height of the retaining walls by a foot and a half and spread topsoil over the hardpan to that depth. I chose the former course. It entailed much hard labor; but something in my peasant soul insisted that it was the more honest course. A peasant is by nature suspicious of beguiling surfaces, having been so often deceived by appearance. Furthermore, he knows that a degree of clay in garden soil is all to the good.

So with a heavy ditchdigger's pick I broke up the hardpan, reduced some of it to powder with blows of the pick and the flat of the shovel, hauled the rest of it away in a wheelbarrow, and brought back in its stead, in the same barrow, the finest kind of humus-rich topsoil. This solution to the problem was made particularly attractive by time and place. Our lot is a corner property, and across the two intersecting streets there was an abundance of "loose" land— land to which someone, perhaps even the county, had title but which was more or less neglected and left unguarded, there being no immediate use for it. It was actually a minor wilderness of conifers, alders, maples, and indigenous shrubs.

There was nowhere a NO TRESPASSING sign. One could fell a tree there for firewood, or take up a small one and root it in one's own land, or remove topsoil for flowerbeds. The owners simply didn't mind. Or they were not around.

The area across one of the streets was a wooded ravine the southern slope of which was, in effect, plowed by gophers, beavers, and rabbits. At the head of every burrow there was a mound of excellent topsoil. As the name suggests, topsoil is surface soil. It is *excellent* topsoil when it is loose, granular, and dark with decayed organic matter. It is normally found in wooded areas untouched by man, where centuries of decaying vegetation have enriched the ground. In his excursions to the country, the amateur gardener should be on the lookout for such loose land. Failing to find it, he must procure from his nurseryman whatever topsoil he may need. Well, I was fortunate in being able to get all I needed in the ravine across the street, giving to the loose land a barrow of hardpan in exchange for every barrow of topsoil I wheeled onto my property.

I did all the work in July a couple of decades ago. This was the pattern of my labor: I broke up the hardpan with repeated thrusts of the pick. The large clumps I loaded onto the wheelbarrow; the smaller ones I pulverized. When the wheelbarrow was full, I wheeled it across the street and dumped the hardpan down the slope of the canyon. Then I loaded the barrow with the fine soil the friendly rodents had heaped for me and wheeled it to the spot on my garden plot whence I had removed the hardpan. By the end of the month the work was done. The substitution of fine soil for hardpan had been achieved at no more cost than the sweat of my brow and an occasional soreness in the muscles of the back. Actually, it was achieved at no cost at all, for I had health and strength and plenty of bread and wine; and the work, heavy though it was, was a pleasure. Barren was converted into productive ground; to those of us who are of the earth, such labor is always pleasant.

I must now tell you about an amusing encounter I had while I filched sweet soil from the canyon slope for my garden. While I was bent to my labor a booming voice called to me from the brink of the ravine, "Don't work too hard, young fellow! Pick and shovel work will kill you in this heat." It was Uncle Harry.

"No danger at all, sir," I replied, unbending myself and mopping my brow. "I am having a bit of fun wheeling dirt."

He was in flannel trousers and white shirt open at the throat. His hands were clasped over his rump. In answer to his questions I told him precisely what I was doing. There was some pride in my telling, and I may have hoped to be complimented for my industry and thrift.

"How long do you figure it will take you?" he asked.

"I don't know exactly. Probably most of the summer."

"With a bulldozer and a dump truck you could do the whole job in less than a day. Shovels and wheelbarrows are things of the past."

"I know," I said, "but I'm not in a hurry. Bulldozers and trucks are no fun. Besides, I enjoy pick-and-shovel work. I like to sweat."

"You can't be serious!"

"The hell I'm not! I am happy when I shovel dirt and the sweat pours from my brow."

"Do you mean to tell me. . . ."

It was no use. We were poles apart. So I let him pontificate while I loaded my wheelbarrow. Before he took his leave he told me that he owned the canyon and the land to the north of it and that he once owned the whole of View Ridge, the name of the residential district in which our house is located. As he moved away, his big hands clasped behind him, I called out to him: "Hey, Uncle Harry! Don't you see that I am moving your property onto my property? Aren't you going to give me hell?"

He shook his head without turning around. Was it his way of saying "No, I am not going to give you hell, take all you want"? Or was he shaking his head in disgust at a fool who preferred a shovel to a bulldozer? I'll never know. Perhaps, with his bulldozer-and-dump-truck mind, he failed to see how much dirt a tough, determined peasant could move in a summer with a shovel and wheelbarrow. Then again, shrewd speculator that he was, already planning to fill the canyon and build houses on the fill, he may have seen that he was getting the better of the bargain. Hardpan is a better foundation than sand, and I was giving him a cubic foot of hardpan for every cubic foot of loose soil I was taking away. Or he may have been a generous man pure and simple, the more generous for owning, at the time, so much loose land.

By the end of July I was as hard as nails, as brown as a nut, and my garden was built.

Just in time! For within a month Uncle Harry was back with his bulldozer and dump truck. And oh! the havoc he has wrought with those diesel-driven demons! There is no more wilderness now to the east of my garden. Where there were once shrubs and evergreens, there are now unattractive houses hastily put together. Better than half of the canyon has been filled and houses built on the fill. There is no more loose land. The sign of the times is NO TRESPASSING. I have no idea where the beavers and the gophers and the rabbits have gone. And Uncle Harry? Armed and guided and motorized, he goes on yearly safaris to Africa.

But I am still here, and my garden is built. Built now and enriched with the waste of twenty-five years of the Pellegrini way of life; a way of life from which waste has been virtually eliminated. Do you smell a paradox? Let me explain.

In a couple of decades I have worked into that 1,500 square feet of ground, with my rake and my shovel, tons of waste organic matter: waste from the kitchen, the cellar, the fireplace, and from the garden itself. In that time I have crushed twelve tons of grapes; after the wine from each crushing was fermented and drawn, the waste was plowed into the garden. All waste from the kitchen is kept in a bucket, and when it is full, the waste is buried in the garden. Wood ashes from a much-used fireplace are raked into the soil. And all organic matter from the garden itself, the inedible bulk of all vegetables, pea and bean vines and corn stalks, all weeds and grass clippings, has been added to the soil. All in all, my educated guess is that in two decades the soil in my garden has been enriched with about thirty tons of organic waste matter. And I am telling you about it as a way of suggesting that you, too, may enrich your garden soil in the same way. Never cast any organic matter away if it can be saved and buried in the garden.

Well, now that you know how this little garden was built, here's how I decided what I would grow in it. One is well advised to proceed from general principles and according to plan even in so trifling a venture as planting a garden. First of all I took account of the fact that we consume a great deal and a wide variety of vegetables; so I planned to keep the garden in production as much of the year as possible. Space and geographical location were limiting factors that had to be considered. The plot was small; rain was abundant; the climate generally mild. So I concentrated on growing those vegetables that would do well in the environment I could provide for them. And of these many, since I lacked space for all, I chose the herbs and vegetables we like most; certain others not readily available at the supermarket; and such others that are at their best when brought directly from the garden to the kitchen. In addition to these, I wanted to experiment with a number of "exotics" that, in theory, could not be grown in our region.

Since our garden is elevated several feet above street level by means of concrete walls, it is not so easily invaded by dogs and their young masters; so I decided to forgo the enclosing fence. It has worked out very well. Even though the garden is conspicuous from the street, there is rarely an invader in it. Instead of a fence, I grew a hedge of trellised berry vines on the west and south sides. On the north side, since it parallels a walk much used by ladies and school children, I planted a row of dahlias and hydrangeas. It was a good move. When these are in bloom, I have seen ladies smile approval and young girls stop to caress a bloom. Along the east boundary, up above the highest wall, I planted two rows of artichokes. When full grown these are tall, bushy, attractive, and they intertwine into a hedge. Very lovely and very fruitful. Perhaps you may want to consider the possibility of hedging in your garden in such a way. You may come up with something strikingly original in the way of mingling ornament and utility.

Let us now have a look at what grows between the hedges. I shall do little else than pass the plants in review, the purpose being to dramatize for you what can be grown in a small garden. Later, in Parts Two and Three, I shall deal with the cultivation of herbs and vegetables in some detail.

The climate where we live is such that the growing season extends from late February, when we normally sow peas and put garlic and shallot bulbs in the ground, to the end of November. This means that the growth of herbs and vegetables, each sown at the proper time, continues for nine months. What is in the garden at Thanksgiving is either still growing or mellowing, and it will be available for use until destroyed by a killing freeze sometime during the winter. Or the freeze may not come at all.

In effect, we who live in such a latitude have two distinct planting seasons: early spring and early summer. If we make use of both and proceed in all our operations with care, we shall have, even on a land area no bigger than mine, two harvests so abundant that there will be a surplus for friends and relatives, even after we have frozen or otherwise conserved against the morrow. But this must not dishearten the prospective gardener who lives in the northern latitudes where the growing season begins in May and ends in September. Within the limits of a single growing season, he may produce on so little a plot of land as mine most of the vegetables the family will need for the year, provided he works with diligence and properly conserves the surplus of those vegetables that can be canned or frozen. Let me give you this example: On a strip of land 3 by 50 feet, one can grow 70 heads of cabbage. A single head may weigh from a few pounds to as many as 15 or 20 pounds. If we take 6 pounds as the average weight for a head of cabbage, one may grow a fifth of a ton on that land area—enough cabbage to provide the family a pound and a half a day for the entire year!

Well, such are the produce potentials of a small plot of land, whether the growing season be five or nine months. The total inventory of our garden is about thirty kinds of vegetables and fourteen kinds of herbs. The herbs I shall deal with in Part Two. As I have said, I begin gardening in February, as soon as the weather is right and the soil dry enough to be tilled. I normally aim at having pea seeds in the ground on Washington's birthday. And at about the same time I plant the bulblets of garlic and shallots, unless these were seeded, as they sometimes are, late in the fall. Somewhat later, around the middle of March, I sow such cold-hardy plants as spring cabbage, turnips, mustard, spinach, onions, rocket, chard, chicory, beets, carrots, and lettuce. Some of these are sown two or three times during the season at intervals of three to four weeks. The process among horticulturists is known as successive sowing; its purpose is to assure a continuous supply of a vegetable while it is prime for the table; its justification is both aesthetic and economic. One cannot eat an eighteen-foot row of lettuce plants if they all mature at the same time. Much will be inevitably wasted. So instead of sowing an eighteen-foot row at one time, one sows a six-foot row every three weeks during all the time that lettuce can be sown. Waste will be reduced to a minimum, and enjoyment increased to the maximum.

The same procedure may be followed for the other vegetables in this first group. Happily, they do not all mature at the same time. Beets sown on the same day with carrots will mature a month earlier, and a first crop of turnips, seeded at the same time as cabbage, will be completely harvested before the first cabbage is ready to eat. No two vegetables require exactly the same time to mature, nor do all plants of the same vegetable in a given seeding attain table maturity at the same time. Thus, a certain spacing of the harvest is structured into the nature of the vegetable itself. These facts of nature are a blessing and spare the gardener the embarrassment of having too many good things on hand at the same time.

There is a difference, too, in the necessary length of the rows. A six-foot row of carrots will yield enough for a dozen dinners, while a six-foot row of spinach will yield enough for only two. Bearing in mind these differences, as well as our relative preferences in vegetables, I plan the length of each row accordingly.

Later in the spring, when the sun has drawn the chill from the ground, I plant peppers, tomatoes, zucchini, cucumbers, and four kinds of beans. Three of these are varieties of green or snap beans; the other is known as a green shell bean. It is harvested as fresh peas are harvested, when the bean is fully developed in the pod but before it dries.

This completes the spring sowing. You will note that there are twenty different vegetables growing, not counting garlic and shallots, which I list as herbs. And to give you a further idea of how much can be produced on such a little plot, I can report that on forty square feet of land I grow better than a hundred pounds of green beans. Add another ten square feet and one may harvest a year's supply of green beans for an average family.

The second sowing begins toward the end of May and ends in mid-August. From mid-July on, some of the land on which the early crops were sown will be vacated. The peas have been harvested, and the spinach, early spring cabbage, and the lettuce, making the areas in which they were grown available for the second planting, a planting which is always attended, for me, by a very special excitement. The vegetables in this group are among my favorites, and they provide a harvest at a time when many vegetable gardens are bare.

Leeks and cardoons I sow in May. Early in July I transplant the celery and set out the plants for the cabbage group: broccoli, purple cauliflower, kale, collards, savoy cabbage, and Brussels sprouts. At about the same time I transplant the endive. And toward the middle of August I sow turnips once more, for harvesting in the fall and early winter. That is the year's final sowing.

You will note that there are six in the cabbage family, a considerable variety of very nutritious and hardy leaf vegetables. How many shall you plant? And what space will they require? I normally set out about ninety plants of the entire cabbage group. The exact number of each is determined by the nature of the plant and our own taste preferences. For example, savoy cabbage and purple cauliflower, both of which we like very much, produce a single head. Once it is cut, that is the end of the plant. Broccoli, kale, and collards proliferate continuously in leaves or buds; when these are cut for the table the plant produces a fresh supply. Therefore, I set out considerably more plants of the former than the latter, but the total is always around ninety. And the space requirement for these? Not much more than 160 square feet! Once again I ask you to note how much can be produced on so little ground.

To demonstrate the hardiness of certain vegetables, and to correct the impression of the many who believe that the end of summer is the end of the garden's fruitfulness, I'll now report on the condition of my garden following a cold spell. About the middle of January, after three weeks of very cold weather for Seattle, I went to the garden to see what damage had been done. There had been snow in December, and for several days the temperature remained at a few degrees below freezing. Then there had been rain; and after the rain the temperature had dropped once more, to three degrees below freezing. Then again, rain. On the day I went into the garden, a heavy morning frost was followed by clear and sunny skies.

I was pleased to note that the severe weather had done no substantial damage to my vegetables. Winter was well under way and more than half of my garden area was in production. Some of the plants had been stung at the outer edges. And no wonder, with the weather as harsh as it had been! But the core, the heart of each plant was untouched. The sting had been fatal to the outer stalks of the artichoke plants, but only because they were frail with age and, in any case, doomed to corruption before spring. The turnips, too, were sound. The fresh, inner leaves had drooped a little in deference to the freezing blast, but they were now once

more lifted to the sun. Similarly stung, but only super-
ficially, were the chard, the chicory, the endive, and the
parsley. Their hardy hearts had taken the freeze in stride.
The leeks and the entire cabbage group were in no way
damaged. The kale, in fact, had been improved by the cold
weather; it had been chastened, sweetened, tenderized. And
the cardoons had fared better in the harsh weather than the
gardener himself. But I had provided them special protection, of which I shall give an account in Chapter 9.

It must be for this reason that I am always a little excited
by the summer sowing for a fall and winter harvest, for no
matter how often one has taken a savoy cabbage or a cauliflower or any other vegetable from under the snow, the
phenomenon always pleases and astonishes. In a world of
well-nigh miraculous achievements in the sciences it seems
a trivial irrelevance, but I rejoice in it!

Let us now have a look at my exotics. And that will conclude the inventory of my garden, except for the herbs,
which I shall deal with in the next chapter. By "exotic" I
mean plants that are not indigenous to this region and that,
theoretically, cannot be grown here. But gardeners of my
stripe and passion are not easily awed by theory. Land for
us is not something to possess but to cultivate. In the in-
scrutable scheme of things, it is Nature's womb in which
are sown the seeds of much that man requires for his nourishment and joy. And when we see a plant that strikes our
fancy, we cannot resist the urge to root it in our own soil
and observe what happens, confident, somehow, that it will
grow for our sake.

And in this empirical approach to nature, with faith in
ourselves and in what we are doing with pick and shovel,
we are curiously like the early Greek philosophers. Thales
of Miletus and his followers had a grand idea that the world
around them could be understood, if one only took the

trouble to observe it properly. Urged on by curiosity, they purged their minds of superstition and preconceptions and looked closely at their world. They wanted to *know*. And so do we want to know. The object of their scrutiny was the universe; of ours, the patch of ground we call our garden. We take note of theory but rely on experiment. We plant, observe, and conclude, and, like the early Greeks, we can be astonished by what we learn.

This curiosity, this passion, this reverence for the soil is something that Uncle Harry, a man of affairs, cannot understand. Three years ago he passed by while I was digging a hole in which to root a plant I had brought up from Southern California.

"And now what are you up to, young fellow?" he asked.

"Nothing much. Just digging a hole in which to plant a loquat."

"A what?"

"A small evergreen malaceous tree, *Eriobotrya japonica,* native to China and Japan."

"And what the hell's that?"

"That," I repeated, "is a loquat. It bears small, yellow, plum-like fruit. Very delicious."

"You say it's from China? Do you think it'll make it here?"

"I don't know," I said. "I am a Greek, a disciple of Thales of Miletus. I want to know."

He went away, shaking his head, complacent in the conviction that I was a nut.

Well, now I do know. A plant that is native to China and Japan will grow here in the Puget Sound country. When I brought the loquat home from sunny California, it was a slip of a yearling a little less than two feet long, without a blemish and green with the desire to grow. I firmed it into the ground, staked it against buffeting winds, gave it food;

and it grew for my sake. It is now well over five feet high; it has several branches; the leaves are large, green, and healthy. It has survived some very harsh weather—gale winds, snow, hail, and freezing blasts. And yet there it is in full vigor, at the top of the west wall of the garden, flanked by rhododendrons. I doubt that there is anywhere a happier loquat than mine.

Will it bear fruit when it is old enough? We shall see. The fig trees do, and the fig, theoretically, is even more out of place here than the loquat. It is a semitropical plant, native to Southwest Asia. I have two: one is at the south end of the west wall and the other at the southwest corner of the house. One bears large, firm, sweet figs blood-red inside; the other bears yellow fruits, not so firm or large but just as sweet.

From late August through September we have an abundance of figs, despite the flock of birds that gorge on them. They are small birds, and we see them only early in the morning when the figs are ripe. They peck and chirp and peck and chirp and awaken us with their fig-muted chirpings. And when there are no more figs, they disappear. Perhaps they are fig peckers from Southwest Asia.

I live in the hope that the birds will never return, but since I know they will, I have made peace with them. The only effective way to protect fruit against birds is altogether inexpedient. One must cover the fruit tree or berry bushes with spreads of some sort of netting, but where the trees are large and the bushes numerous, this measure becomes impractical. So we must make peace with the birds by growing enough fruit for them and for ourselves. The alternative to peace is war—with an automatic shotgun.

Figs and peaches ripen at the same time, and our peach tree is conveniently located midway between the two fig trees. It is another of my exotics, for the peach, like the fig, is a hot-country plant. And it, too, grows for my sake. This is the second peach tree; the first became sterile in 1964. Weary with bearing big luscious crops, it bore no more. So I took it up root and all and cast it mercilessly into the fire, quoting Scripture to ease my conscience: *Every tree that bringeth not forth good fruit is hewn down and cast into the fire.*

And on the same day, in the selfsame hole I planted another peach. It was four years old; it is now nine and bearing furiously.

At the same time that I brought the loquat from California, I brought another exotic, a bay tree, *Laurus nobilis,* the European culinary laurel. It was a mere slender switch about eighteen inches long. It is now more than four feet high and has developed many branches. It has grown more slowly than the loquat, but that must be its nature, for it has grown well. It has endured the same harsh winters as the loquat. I know, therefore, that it is happy and well established in its new environment. There it is, for everyone to see, above the west wall of the garden, a few feet from one of the fig trees.

And near the other fig tree is another bay, the *Umbellularia californica.* It is commonly known as the California bay and grows in profusion in the Big Sur country. I read about it years ago in the poems of Robinson Jeffers and assumed that it was the culinary laurel. I wondered then whether the tree would grow in my garden, and then forgot about it until Thanksgiving day in 1956. I was walking in the woods above Partington Ridge, about fifty miles south of Carmel. *Umbellulariae* were all around me! I took up a little one, trimmed it to a size that would fit in my suitcase, since I was traveling by train, and took it to the home of the friends with whom I was celebrating Thanksgiving. We kept the tiny roots in moist soil, and when I left we wrapped them in well-soaked moss with outer wrappings of newspapers and cloth and tucked the little *Umbellularia* in my suitcase. Five days after I had taken it from its habitat in the Big Sur woods, it was planted on the level above my garden about ten feet away from the fig tree. It was the end of November.

There were several leaves on it and they held on through the winter, but the little slip of a tree showed no sign of new life the following spring. I had patience and coaxed it along, for I, too, had been transplanted when very young and knew what it meant to feed on foreign soil. My patience was rewarded: the second spring it began to grow. It has now become, miraculously, twins, each trunk better than two inches in diameter. It has grown no faster than the *Laurus nobilis,* but it is just as sound and, I am quite certain, just as happy in its new environment.

I now hope to add a medlar tree, *Mespilus germanica,* to my group of exotics. It is a small malaceous tree, related to the loquat. Its fruit resembles the crab apple and is edible only in the early stages of decay. I shall have one quite soon —and it will grow for my sake.

On this confident note, I end the inventory of my garden. Nor have I done with experimenting in growing what is good and what is lovely. You may have been amazed to learn how much of what is good and lovely can be grown on so small a patch of ground. However, it was not my intention to amaze you. I have taken you on a tour of my garden to make you confident that you may equal or surpass what I have done. Have you the disposable land? Have you the will? And that little bit of gluttony in your nature that makes you rejoice in the harvest?

And now let us talk of herbs.

PART TWO
Of the Lovely Aromatics

F O U R

Herbs Are the Soul
of Cookery

To say that herbs are the soul of cookery is to affirm, metaphorically, a culinary truth: their judicious and imaginative
use in the kitchen results in a distinguished, sophisticated
cuisine. Don't be discouraged by the words "distinguished"
and "sophisticated"; such a cuisine is easily within your
competence. Submit yourself to a very simple test: roast half
a chicken with herbs—I shall show you in the Epilogue how
this is done—and roast the other half without them. Now
smell and taste the two parts. You smile with approval! You
glow with culinary confidence! The seasoned part smells
and tastes better than the other! Your cuisine is now distinguished and sophisticated. And wasn't it all very simple?
The judicious and imaginative use of herbs did the trick.
Voilà!

Is it any wonder, then, that in Europe and the Orient,
where the use of herbs in cooking is as common as the use
of salt and pepper, there should be a mythology of herbs,
a veritable herb lore, just as there is a mythology, a lore of
wine? It is, indeed, so extensive and so diverse, ranging
from the romantic to the pathological, that it would require

volumes to anthologize the best of it. Much of the lore, particularly the anecdotal material accepted as knowledge, has its genesis more in desire than in experience: rosemary leaves strewn under the bed will prevent bad dreams; munching caraway seeds will bring a bloom to the cheeks of pale-faced maidens; garlic juice in the nostrils is a safeguard against the plague; a sprig of anise tied to the bedpost will make one look young in the morning; an indifferent face may be made fair by washing it with an infusion of white wine and rosemary leaves. There is, of course, no proof for these quaint and interesting claims. Wine is a good and pleasant thing, and sweet basil will do wonders to fettuccine. From these facts it is an easy leap to the wish-conclusion that herbs and wine are rich in miraculous virtues. Nor is such wishful thinking regrettable. There is, in fact, much good in it, for it affirms in many delightful ways that wine and herbs relate very closely to the aesthetic in man's nature, his desire for that which is pleasant.

And that which is pleasant, all that contributes to purely sensuous pleasures, all that urges one to abandon Calvin and follow Epicurus and seek a measure of redemption in joyous living has been for too long suspect in an America that was forged in the Puritan ethic. The Anglo-Saxons owe their culinary heritage of mashed potatoes and somber gravy to the teachers and preachers, statesmen and philosophers whose *busyness* and austerity fashioned that essentially gloomy and stern view of life. A dish that smelled good and tasted even better than it smelled, and so was eaten with fresh appetite and heightened pleasure, would certainly stimulate appetites of another sort and urge one on to pleasures more visceral, especially if the savory food were accompanied by a glass of wine. And that would spell damnation. So boil the potatoes and water the roast, and fill the dinner goblets with water, and let each one rejoice in the austere pursuit of business.

It was a cruel philosophy rooted in the Middle Ages and supported by a misreading of the Sacred Book. It attempted to legislate out of existence certain wholesome appetites of the flesh, man's instinctive search for those experiences that yield immediate pleasure, and, in the long pull, it failed. Prohibition is out; gourmet cooking and wine are in. In the America of today the view of life fostered by the Puritan ethic has been purged of much of its sobriety. Many, many Americans have made the happy discovery that there is neither sin nor wickedness in a sprig of rosemary and a glass of wine; that, other things being equal, a sophisticated cuisine, by increasing total contentment, is more likely to promote the good than the bad life. And this sane trend in America's coming of age is attested by the growing interest in a sophisticated cuisine, in wine as the indispensable dinner beverage, and in herbs as "the very soul of good cookery." I owe the phrase to Marcellina, about whom I shall have something to say later.

Culinary herbs! the lovely aromatics! The secret of good cookery is in the use of these. And since they are not generally available at the supermarket, you must grow them yourself. For the dry herbs, in the very process of drying, lose their spicy essence; at best, they are only an inadequate substitute for the fresh. I shall tell you more about them, how the best of them may be grown and used, but first, a word about my own interest in herbs. The intent here is to dramatize as vividly as I can the statement that fresh herbs, the lovely aromatics, are indeed the soul of cookery.

It is my good fortune that I was born in Italy, of peasant parents who were both good cooks, and in a culture where the pleasures of the table were applauded even by the clergy. How well I remember the corpulent, rosy-cheeked parish priest sitting at our table and drinking a toast to Mother's savory broth! A dish of good food, whether it was a soup, a stew, a vegetable, a fish, was the preoccupation of everyone. They openly exulted in it, talked about it, named the flavoring agent that gave it character, or suggested how it might have been improved with a little less x and a bit more y. When they sat together in the evening knitting or mending, housewives talked frequently about cookery, wondering with what herbs and condiment they might contrive a good dish out of the lowly raw materials they had to work with. They sometimes disagreed on what herbs and spices should be used to flavor a dish of frogs, for example, and then there would be a spirited discussion in which even the men and older children participated. Everyone was interested in eating well, and no one even faintly suspected that delicious food would nudge one toward damnation.

In such an environment I passed my early childhood. Then we emigrated to America, where, with an abundance of good raw materials at their disposal, my parents—Father usually cooked on Sundays—achieved a very fine cuisine. Every dinner was in some way distinguished, and its "secret," known to every French and Italian housewife, was the use of fresh herbs.

Since I was very young and very busy with the myriad interests of the young, I took my culinary good fortune pretty much for granted. Until I went away to college. Then I realized that when I had moved from our home in the country and gone to Seattle I had left behind a very fine cuisine the like of which I could not find in the university community. And no wonder! The entire state, the whole Northwest, had not yet discovered garlic! But I *must* find it, I told myself. I *must* have an occasional dinner such as I had enjoyed at home.

And find it I did in the homes of Italian immigrants in Seattle's "Little Italy." Even before I had finished with registration, I began my exploration of the Italian commu-

nity, intent on cultivating the friendship of some of the
then youngish housewives who were reputed to be good
cooks. Within a year I was on "family" terms with more
than a dozen good cooks. Some were from the north of Italy;
some from the central provinces; two were from the south.
They all had large kitchen gardens in which they grew their
herbs and vegetables. Excited by the abundance they had
found in America, they were all intent on perfecting their
cuisine. They consulted with one another, exchanged ideas,
and sometimes resolutely disagreed on whether a certain
herb was essential in preparing a dish.

Since I was frequently in the home of one or the other of
them when they visited in the evening after dinner, I learned
a great deal from them about cookery and the use of herbs.
Occasionally I was on hand while one of them was preparing dinner; then I would observe and ask questions. And
when I went home I would tell Mother about some of the
dishes I had eaten and liked; she, delighted with my interest
in cookery, would tell me how she prepared the same dish.
In this way I learned that the secret of a fine cuisine was
the use of fresh herbs and that without them, food could
be made good enough to eat, but never good enough to in-
spire praise.

The two best cooks I met in Seattle's "Little Italy" happened to be neighbors. Let me simply call them Angelina
and Marcellina. They were also good gardeners. I was
fascinated by these two women because in addition to being
good cooks, they were strikingly different in character and
bound to each other by a subtle, silent culinary competition.
Each was certain that she was the better of the two, and
when they talked about cookery, the intent was somehow to
get this point across without seeming to do anything of the
sort. Of that good-humored competition I was the happy
beneficiary, for when one learned that the other had made

fettuccine for me, she promptly invited me to dinner and gave me fettuccine made *her* way. "Are they good?" she would ask as she watched me eat them with my customary groaning sort of relish. And without waiting for a reply she would add, with the subtlest touch of irony, "Of course, Marcellina [Angelina] makes them better." With a wink, a gesture, an ambiguous raising of the brows, but without speaking a word, I had to praise the one without seeming to betray the other.

Angelina was from Tuscany, the land of Italy's finest olive oil; Marcellina was from Parma, the land of butter and cheese. The one used olive oil exclusively in her cookery; the other used much butter. And they often argued about which was the better fat for cooking. Marcellina dressed her fettuccine with butter, cheese, and fresh basil, an herb for which she had a special affection. When it was in season she often carried a sprig of it with her for sniffing when she went visiting. Angelina insisted that the best dressing for fettuccine was the classic meat sauce used for spaghetti. In preparing a roasting chicken for the oven, Marcellina insisted that Angelina was wrong in adding celery leaves to certain other herbs. And so they argued, and each looked to me for support of her views. I ate heartily the proof of their theories and somehow managed to keep them both happy and cooking for me.

It was in listening to their talk about cookery that I became aware, for the first time, that in speaking of herbs the Italian housewives generally used the word *odorini*. It is the endearing plural diminutive of the Italian word *odore,* "odor." Thus, *odorini* may be literally translated as the "dear little odors or fragrances." Angelina and Marcellina, chatting about culinary herbs, revealed their affectionate regard for them by using the term. "Lovely aromatics" is a fairly good translation, and there is no doubt that they are the soul of cookery. On this point, Angelina and Marcellina were in complete agreement.

FIVE

The Herb Family

What is an herb? The word itself derives from the Latin *herba,* which means grass. In botany "herb" is the name given to those plants the stem or stalk of which dies down to the root each year and does not become, as in shrubs and trees, woody and permanent. Such plants are called herbaceous. Among the many varieties of herbs, some are herbaceous and some are not; some are annuals, some biennials, and some are perennials. A considerable number have a well-established culinary value; others are noted primarily for their medicinal, cosmetic, or ornamental virtues. In the interest of precision, then, it is advisable to use the differentiating terms: culinary herbs, medicinal herbs, cosmetic herbs, and ornamental herbs, it being understood that some herbs may possess two or more of these virtues. Thus what Italian housewives, with considerable license, call *odorini,* we, with more precision, shall call culinary herbs. Of these there are several dozen, some indispensable in sophisticated cookery, others with little culinary merit. We must therefore make a subjective judgment and choose among them those that have the most utility for the home gardener whose sole interest in herbs is the improvement of his cuisine. Accordingly, we shall take a quick glance at the various herb families, and in the next chapter we shall deal with the cultivation and use of the several herbs that any accomplished chef would consider indispensable in the kitchen.

Culinary herbs constitute a "family" only in the sense that they are related by their established culinary virtues. In a strict botanical sense, every herb is a member of a plant family. What follows is a brief description of the several plant families to which most culinary herbs belong. It is well to know this in order to see herbs in their proper botanical perspective.

THE LILY FAMILY (*Liliaceae*). In this group of plants there are about 200 species. Most of them are herbaceous. Of the few culinary herbs that belong to this family, *Allium sativum,* garlic, *Allium schoenoprasum,* chives, and *Allium ascalonicum,* shallots, would be listed as indispensable by all chefs. *Allium porrum,* leek, and *Allium tuberosum,* Oriental garlic, also belong to this family. The latter is a chive-like plant with rather small bulbs that have a flavor more mild than garlic. The leek I consider a vegetable, for it is more often eaten as a vegetable than used as a flavoring agent. Accordingly, I shall deal with it in Part Three.

THE BUCKWHEAT FAMILY (*Polygonaceae*). This family is about one third the size of the lily group. *Rumex scutatus,* French sorrel, is the best culinary herb in the group. It is more frequently used as a potherb than as a condiment. One has perhaps heard of the well-known sorrel soup of France.

THE PARSLEY FAMILY (*Umbelliferae*). Most of the plants in this family are herbaceous, and more than a dozen are culinary herbs. It is fitting that the best known of these, the most universally used, parsley, *petroselinum crispum,* should bear the name of the family to which it belongs. *Anethum graveolens,* dill, because of its wide use in pickling cucumbers, is probably as well known as parsley. *Anthriscus cerefolium,* chervil, also known as beaked parsley, looks very much like parsley, is used in much the same way, and deserves to be better known. *Carum carvi,* caraway, *Coriandrum sativum,* coriander, and *Cuminum cyminum,* cumin, are plants grown primarily for their seeds, but these are readily available on any spice shelf and the home gardener may not want to bother with them. The same may be said of *Foeniculum vulgare,* fennel, and *Pimpinella anisum,* anise, although the fresh leaves of fennel have considerable culinary use. Another variety of fennel, *Foeniculum vulgare dulce,* known at the market as Florence fennel, is grown like celery and is a vegetable rather than a culinary herb.

THE MINT FAMILY (*Labiatae*). This family takes its botanical name from the fact that most of the plants in it have a bilabiate, two-lipped corolla. Nearly a third of the better-known culinary herbs belong to this family, and if we agree that there are twelve culinary herbs that are indispensable to good cookery and ought to be in every kitchen garden, more than half of them belong to the mint family: *Majorana hortensis,* sweet marjoram; *Origanum vulgare,* wild marjoram (oregano); *Thymus vulgaris,* garden thyme; *Mentha pulegium,* English pennyroyal; *Ocimum basilicum,* sweet basil; *Rosmarinus officinalis,* rosemary; *Salvia officinalis,* sage; and, of course, *Mentha spicata,* spearmint, the best of the several varieties of mint. To this group there also belongs the much used in the kitchen and delightfully named *Satureia hortensis,* summer savory.

THE COMPOSITE FAMILY (*Compositae*). In this, the largest family of seed-bearing plants, there is only one culinary herb that interests us, but it is very important: *Artemisia dracunculus,* tarragon.

This gives us better than two dozen culinary herbs valuable in cookery, some much more so than others. There are many more, but their culinary use is limited. For example, rue, lemon verbena, tansy, and hyssop, while they are occasionally used in the kitchen, are better known for their medicinal properties. A tea made of lemon verbena is reputed to be "febrifugal, stomachic, antispasmodic, and antiflatulent." Rue is not only an aid in the relief of flatulence; a bouquet of its leaves and flowers, placed in a bed, will repel bedbugs. And a nicely brewed hyssop tea is both an aperient and a laxative. Where does your interest in herbs end?

Assuming that you want to grow as many of the above culinary herbs as you can, I suggest you divide your garden into two sections, one for herbs and one for vegetables. Plan with care and tailor the division to your sense of color and design. Begin with a list of the herbs you want to grow. Keep in mind the size, shape, and color of each plant. Remember that rosemary, sage, thyme, oregano, and tarragon are perennial. Once planted, cultivated, and kept properly in trim, these are permanent plantings; place them in your garden accordingly. The annuals, such as garlic, shallots, and parsley, should be rotated; plant them in a different area, though perhaps in the same general location, each season. And don't forget this basic horticultural principle: every plant requires a certain space, the measure of which is the maximum spread of its leaves or branches at maturity. Do not be misled by the size of the seed. A borage seed is nearly microscopic, but the plant is two feet tall and has a branch spread of eighteen inches. And you know all about the acorn!

I myself do not have what could be properly called an herb garden. Of the herbs I consider necessary in our cuisine, some are in the garden proper; others are tucked away in various places on the upper level among the flowering shrubs. The two perennials I prize particularly, rosemary and sage, are hardy enough, but near-zero weather may destroy them. To minimize the possibility of losing them, I have several plants of each growing in various places, some in areas more protected than others. The hope is that one or more of each will survive any likely disaster. And since rosemary is more vulnerable to severely cold weather than sage, I have potted two plants of it.

Potting. What is it? How and why is it done? Growing plants in flowerpots or other containers is known as potting. There are three reasons for potting: one may simply want potted plants in the house; he may have no spot of land on which to grow them outside; or he may want to bring them inside when killing weather is imminent. In the next chapter I shall indicate the general weather requirements of each herb; I can say at this point, however, that none of the better-known biennials and perennials will survive subzero weather. It is the responsibility of each gardener to ascertain which will and which will not survive the winter in his region, and then proceed accordingly.

If you live where near or below-zero temperatures are normal, plan on potting some of your herbs. If you have space indoors, you can grow your herbs in a windowbox. Or you may grow them in ordinary flowerpots or in square

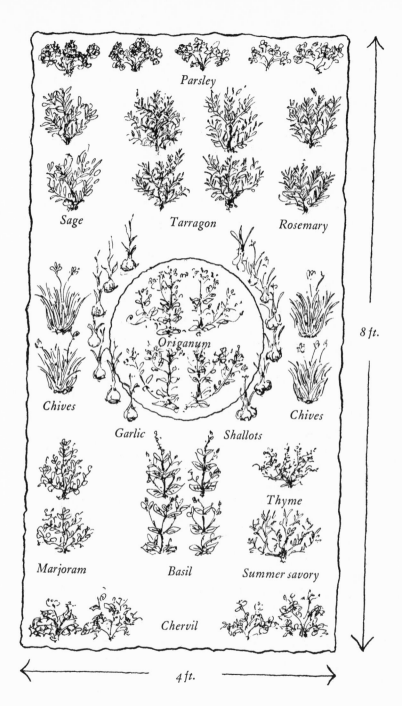

Parsley

Sage   Tarragon   Rosemary

Chives   Origanum   Chives

Garlic   Shallots

Marjoram   Basil   Thyme

Summer savory

Chervil

8 ft.

4 ft.

boxes at least a foot deep and made of some durable wood such as cedar or redwood. For rosemary and sage, the container should be about fifteen inches in diameter and eighteen inches deep; for other herbs a container the size of a water bucket will do. When thus potted the plants can be kept outside until the severe weather sets in. When they are brought inside, they must be watered regularly and kept where they will get plenty of air and daylight, preferably on an enclosed sun porch or near a window.

There is an alternative to potting: plant the herbs in the garden, and at the onset of winter dig them up and bring them inside. In digging them up, follow this procedure: water the plant well several hours before it is to be dug up. This will firm the soil into a compact ball around the entire root system. If the spread of the branches interferes with your work, tie them in a bundle. Your objective now is to take the plant from the ground without disturbing the roots, so you must first determine the lateral spread of the root system by some careful preliminary digging. From that point dig in a circle around the stem. Measuring from the ends of the longest roots, the hole should be about ten inches wide and deep enough to get well under the deepest root. When this is done, work burlap or canvas around and under the root clump, bring the ends together, and secure them tightly around the stem. You have now isolated the plant from the ground and wrapped its entire root system into a tight ball. Take it up, put it in any ordinary box, bring it inside, and give it the winter care prescribed in the last paragraph for potted plants.

In this way even large trees, with the aid of machinery, can be safely moved. All things considered, and especially for the shrub herbs such as rosemary and sage, it is the more practical method of protecting plants from killing weather. Let them grow to whatever size; the work of taking them

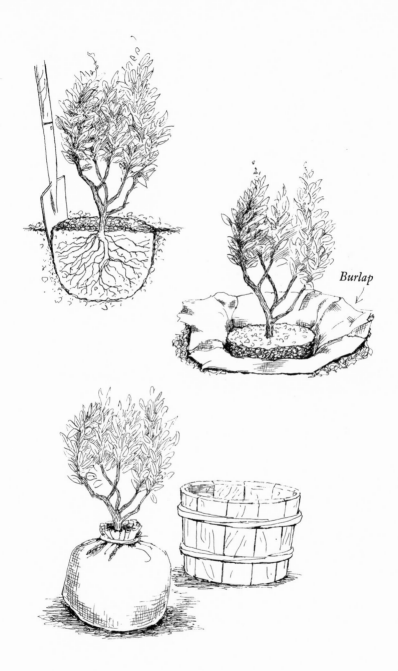

Burlap

up from the ground and doing the job well will be a pleasant challenge.

In the next chapter I shall deal with the cultivation and use of a dozen indispensable herbs. As for others that may take your fancy, remember that no one of them has a definitive use. By continual experimentation, you will discover that certain nuance of flavor that a given aromatic will contribute to a dish and that pleases the palate. Once such a discovery has been made, there will be heightened pleasure at your table; and pleasure in dining is what we seek.

Before we proceed with the next chapter and a closer look at the more useful culinary herbs, we must take note of a group of plants that are known as wild potherbs. The reason for grouping these together and differentiating them from the others is that they are really vegetables; their use as flavoring agents is limited. All of them are edible. Many are common weeds. Some are native to certain regions in North America; others were introduced from the Old World. The better known are the following: *Urtica,* nettles, of which there are several species; *Rumex acetosa,* sour dock, also known as sorrel; *Chenopodium album,* pigweed or lamb's-quarters; *Portulaca oleracea,* purslane; *Brassica kaber,* field mustard; *Rorippa Nasturtium officinale,* watercress; *Chicorium intybus,* chicory; *Taraxacum officinale,* dandelion.

Practically all of these and others will be known to octogenarians and older people; the young generation may know one or two. The reason is that people who were born six and more decades ago are likely to have known hunger; and hunger drives one to pasture, compels one to explore the total environment for food. The young generation are creatures of the affluent society; they forage in the supermarkets, where there are no weeds for sale.

Well, in the way of food, their loss is not regrettable. I

have tried a number of the wild potherbs, lavished on them all my meager culinary talents, and with results not particularly memorable. Four of them, properly prepared for the table, are excellent: wild mustard, sorrel, Canadian thistle, and dandelion. These I have found so good and eat them so regularly that I must be permitted to sing in praise of one of them.

First, however, a final word about all food from the wilderness. There is a tendency to romanticize that which is wild. Perhaps the vestigial brute in us yearns to go back to nature. I have convinced myself, however, that one who can have spinach is well advised to leave nettles to rot in the sour, humid soil in which they grow; and he who is blessed with an abundance of beef had better hold his fire and let elk and deer and moose ruminate in peace to their natural end in the forest primeval. There are many upland birds that are better than fowl, but I have had wild ducks and geese that should have been left to quack and honk to the last of their days in peace. I was once a grim hunter and fisherman along with other pioneers who hunted and fished from necessity; I brought to our table every creature that I could capture with gun and trap and hook.

When I was a hungry lad in the Old World, I was even on the verge of becoming a chicken thief, but I was rescued from evil when my father emigrated to become a section hand for the Northern Pacific Railroad. That put an end to hunger, and with dire need no longer a driving motive, I abandoned the wilderness, put away gun and fishing rod, and took up shovel and hoe. The vestigial brute in me that yearns to return to nature finds its fulfillment in the garden. Anyway, friends who hunt and fish keep us well supplied with game. Game fish is always a delight, and with our stock of culinary herbs we can turn much of the rest to good account.

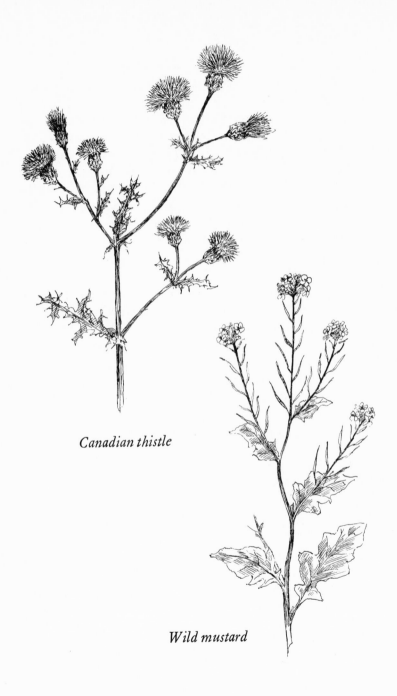

Canadian thistle

Wild mustard

In the spring, however, I hunt wild mustard; the Canadian thistle, which Italians call wild cardoon; and the lowly dandelion. Lowly not only because it is low-growing, its leaves tending to rest on the soil, but also because of all the wild potherbs it is the least proud, the least fussy in choosing where it will make its home. On both sides of, or even on, the tracks, it will take root and live happily. Thus one may find it growing on concrete and asphalt; in sand, gravel, clay, and humus; on lawns, in flower gardens and vegetable patches; in sun or shade or any spot where there

Dandelion

is the slightest moisture. Its inherent gregariousness makes it the most ubiquitous of wild potherbs. No spot of ground, however forbiddingly staked or clearly reserved for roses or rhododendrons or rhubarb, is safe from its guileless intrusion. It comes early, and it comes to stay. And for precisely these reasons, it is universally despised.

But not by me! I welcome its intrusion among my artichokes, cardoons, and savoy cabbages. I cultivate it and weed it and breed it, so that each spring I may have my fill of dandelion, cooked and raw, without having to filch it in the dark of night from the neighbor's lawn. And then I wonder how a weed must feel when it enters the domain of a gardener who weeds it and breeds it to a more luxuriant weediness!

Everyone in the family likes a dandelion salad. We are addicted to it as others are addicted to more noxious weeds. We crave it so much that the first day on which we have it in the spring is made memorable thereby. In our region the first dandelion usually appears about a month before the formal advent of spring, and the season lasts through March. Thereafter, the stem of the flower bud begins to lengthen, and the leaves become too tough and too bitter to be used for salads. So long as the buds are practically stemless and form·a compact cluster at the center of the little plant, the dandelion is edible raw; it is then in its prime and at its best.

During recent years we have made an occasion of our first dandelion salad by having it on Washington's Birthday. While the neighbors proclaim their love of country by unfurling the flag, I do reverence to the land that gives me bread by gathering dandelion greens for our holiday dinner. It has become a symbolic act. Every little plant taken from the mulch, with its bleached, bitter-sweet core, is a reminder of the rich harvest our family gathered in the New Land.

And the dressing itself, too, is such a reminder, for there

is no need now to stint on the ingredients. We can well afford the best of whatever is necessary to dress a salad, thanks to my father's inspired emigration years ago! There are, of course, several salad dressings, but the best of them all, the classic dressing, is that composed of wine vinegar, olive oil, salt, freshly ground pepper, and the scent of garlic. All other dressings for a green salad are but attempts at refinement.

The quality of the olive oil and wine vinegar, the proportion of the condiments, and the amount of dressing for a given bowl of salad greens: these are the important factors to keep in mind in making a salad dressing. If you are unacquainted with olive oil and wine vinegar, go to a reputable gourmet shop and with the aid of the dealer procure the best. Vinegar and oil of poor quality will ruin a salad.

What we are seeking in making the oil-and-vinegar dressing is such a balance between the two that neither dominates the mixture. Too much or too little of either one spells ruin. There must be enough vinegar to cut the oiliness of the oil, and enough oil to soften the acidity of the vinegar, so that the two combined produce a liquid that is smooth and pleasant on the palate. And this is accomplished when the finest wine vinegar and the best olive oil are used in the proportion of one to three respectively.

Assuming now that we have a salad bowl full of young, tender dandelion greens, we are ready for the dressing. Pour one part wine vinegar and three parts olive oil into a small jar, add enough salt and freshly ground pepper, shake thoroughly, and pour the mixture over the greens. Rub two slices of well-toasted bread on both sides with juicy cloves of garlic; cut the toast into croutons, add them to the greens, then mix the salad thoroughly.

The scent of garlic can be added to the salad in other ways. The bowl can be rubbed with garlic; a clove or two can be forced through a garlic press into the dressing; or the garlic can be finely minced and added to the greens. I prefer to do it in the way I have described, for I enjoy eating the garlic-scented croutons, flavored with the dressing, along with the salad greens.

And now a word about the amount of dressing to use for a bowl of dandelion greens, for it is as important to use the correct amount of dressing as it is to use the right proportion of vinegar to oil. Salad greens such as dandelion, chicory, and endive are a little more firm, less watery, and more bitter than the leaves of ordinary lettuce. They require plenty of dressing; and the dressing is sufficient when the greens are given all they can absorb without losing their crispness. Every shred of dandelion should be moist with the dressing, but there should not be so much of it that the crisp, tender leaves are drenched with it.

Pardon this slight digression from the theme of culinary herbs, but the lowly dandelion is worthy of it. And did you know that in mineral and vitamin content it excels all other greens? Bread and cheese, a huge salad of dandelion with oil and vinegar dressing, and a bottle of creamy ale: make a dinner of these and you will explode with vitality!

The Indispensable Dozen

The title of this chapter indicates a subjective judgment. And so it is; nor do I state it with any diffidence. Of the several dozen culinary herbs, I have chosen the following for special praise: garlic, sage, parsley, chervil, tarragon, sweet marjoram, wild marjoram, basil, rosemary, thyme, English pennyroyal, and shallots. I stand pat on the selection, but I must say something in further elucidation of it.

The selection is the result of my own experience in the garden and in the kitchen. Note that I have not included in the list the bay laurel, since that is a tree, or plants such as coriander and caraway, because their value as condiments is primarily in the dry seed. Furthermore, I have excluded herbaceous plants that are often used as seasonings but are not strictly culinary herbs: celery, onion, carrot, chard. These are used as herbs in soups, stews, and sauces, but they are normally eaten as vegetables. Thus, my list of indispensables would be somewhat longer if I had not limited myself to plants that are strictly culinary herbs.

Let us now have a close look at each one of them, beginning with garlic. When garlic is full-grown, it is a compound bulb, a tight cluster of bulblets, or cloves, each enclosed in its own skin. The bulbs and cloves vary in size. A bulb the size of a lemon may be composed of as many as twenty small cloves; a bulb the size of an apple may contain only ten cloves, each the size of an almond in the shell. The second is the size preferred in the kitchen, as I shall explain.

Propagation of garlic is by individual bulblet, or clove. In the North, South, and throughout California, cloves may be put in the ground from early December to very early spring, the season when one normally puts daffodil and other bulbs in the ground. In regions where the temperature drops below zero, garlic should be planted in the spring as soon as the ground can be worked. As in the daffodil bulb, germination proceeds when the weather is too cold for most other plants; so a clove put into the ground around Thanksgiving will be a little plant three or four inches high in mid-January. It will be hardy, capable of surviving snow and such cold temperatures as stay well above zero. By the end of May the leaves and the stem, about eighteen inches long, will be full-grown. Thereafter, for about six weeks, these will gradually degenerate, turning yellow and drying, and the bulb will grow to its full size. The plant must be weeded, cultivated occasionally if the soil around the bulb tends to harden, and kept well watered. During the three final weeks, when it is obvious that the leaves are full-grown and are beginning to age, it will help the bulb to achieve maximum size if the leaves and stem are lodged gently with the foot. This bit of cruelty will hasten leaf degeneration and leave all nutrients for the bulb. When it is full-grown, usually toward the middle of July, it is taken up, dried in the sun for a few days, and then stored in a cool, ventilated place.

Garlic is not too fussy in its soil requirements. However, while it will grow in soils of indifferent quality, it will realize all its potential in soils that are light, well drained,

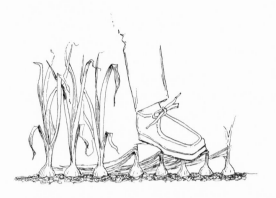

Lodging

and fertile. Cloves are set, root end down, about five inches apart and covered with an inch or so of soil. Where there are several rows, they should be spaced twelve inches apart.

One who knows his garlic wants large, well-formed, juicy cloves. A clove of garlic is sometimes used whole; it is minced, sliced, or put through a press; it is often rubbed on, as on toasted bread or along the inside of a salad bowl; or its juice is scraped with the edge of a knife onto meat, as on a steak or chop. Especially for the latter uses, large cloves are generally more satisfactory, more easily peeled, more easily handled. And a single large clove is often all one needs to flavor the sauce.

To procure large cloves, I practice what in animal husbandry is called selective breeding. Every harvest season I set aside for seed the largest bulbs, composed of large, well-formed cloves. When at the farmer's market or at the home of an accomplished Italian gardener I come upon an exceptional bulb, I add it to my stock. My reward is yearly harvests of garlic as fine as I have seen anywhere. The compound bulbs, rather uniform in size, are composed of ten or twelve large cloves.

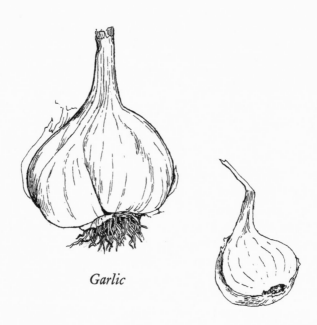

Garlic

In our family we use one bulb a week, about a clove a day. Each harvest season I select enough prize bulbs to give me 60 cloves. These I put into the ground at the proper time and in the manner described; my yearly harvest is 60 bulbs, better than 600 cloves. Since all we need to keep the family in a permanently aromatized state are 365 cloves a year, we always have enough on hand to give to a neighbor who at the very last moment discovers that he has no garlic for his garlic bread.

Garlic bread! This but suggests the many uses of garlic. Rub it lightly on well-toasted bread. Put the bread in a soup bowl, scatter some Parmesan cheese on it and a bit of freshly ground pepper, then fill the bowl with chicken broth and eat it with leisured eagerness as a foundation for your dinner. Or spread the garlic-scented bread with butter and eat it with a piece of your favorite cheese. Try a clove in your hashed browned potatoes, done slowly in good olive oil. Mince a clove and brown it in oil or butter and then sauté blanched, finely chopped spinach in the fat. Add to the list of its uses as you please. Along with shallots and parsley, garlic is the cause of excellence in many sauces, roasts, stews, and soups.

It also has indubitable medicinal virtues. It is an expectorant, a diaphoretic, an antiseptic, a rubefacient. Does that take care of you? It is also very good for the nerves and to keep the blood coursing briskly through the veins. When a flu epidemic threatens, stuff your nose with crushed garlic, anoint your chest with its juice, and go boldly about your business. You will be virus-proof; none shall accost you.

So much for garlic, the universal herb, known and used on all the continents. Grow it yourself, breed it to your taste, and learn about its many uses through continual experimentation. Remember in cultivating it that its life cycle is long. Put in the ground in January, it is harvested seven months later. Don't be tempted to take it up when the plant is a foot long and seems ready to harvest. The compound bulb requires time to develop fully. Have patience.

In preparing a chicken for the oven, Angelina always used plenty of sage, that perennial shrub native to the Mediterranean. In its way of life it is not at all fastidious. It simply wants to grow; but it will grow best where it has nourishment, space, and sun. It is virtually an evergreen and it renews its leaves in the spring. In regions where temperatures do not drop below 15° or 20° F. the leaves endure deep into the winter. Naturally, they are not so juicy and spicy as the fresh leaves, but they are quite adequate and available for use until the new growth appears. In areas where the temperature drops to near and below zero, sage is better potted according to instructions given in the preceding chapter.

When the plant is in its prime, toward the end of spring, the leaves are large, about the size and shape of a bay leaf, a pale green, healthy and strong in spicy odor. What a pity that it and all other living things that are good must pass their prime so quickly!

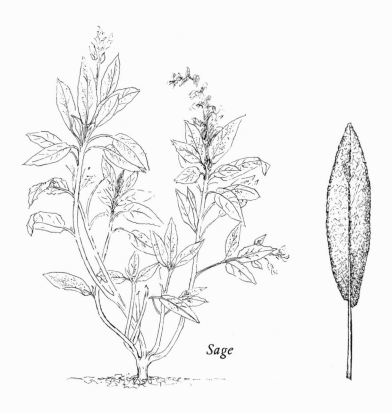

Sage

It is a shrub that grows rapidly. Propagation is by layers, cuttings, plant division, and seeds. There are several varieties. One has reddish leaves; another, the more common, has gray-green leaves. There are also a broad-leaved and a narrow-leaved variety. "Holt's Mammoth" is highly recommended for the home garden.

Sage grows to about two feet high, with a circular spread of about thirty inches. If the plant is started from seed in the spring, thin when the plant is four to six inches high. Transplanting is not necessary. The full-grown leaves are about an inch wide at the center and two to three inches long. They are ready to use in the kitchen when they are half that size or even smaller. However, don't kill the young plant by taking all its leaves before it is well established and has several branches.

It is wise to renew the plant every five or six years, for two reasons. The sage shrub develops a great deal of dead wood, thickly matted underneath the branch tips on which the leaves are borne; in time one has much more unproductive wood than leaf-bearing branches. The shrub is then unpleasing to the eye and its leaves are not as desirable as those of a younger plant. The other reason for renewing the plant is that an older plant goes to seed more quickly than a young one, and consequently its leaves deteriorate sooner. There are fewer of them and they have less sap.

My own sage I brought from my mother's garden twenty-five years ago. She had an enormous clump of it growing against the fence that once enclosed the chicken yard. In the spring it was a sight, a gently domed carpet of large green leaves, an aromatic embodiment of early spring and nature in full regeneration. It was a joy to look at and smell a crushed leaf and contemplate its many uses. I took from it a well-rooted branch in February and put it in the ground in my garden; and there it is still, the parent plant from which

I have started so many others, for ourselves and for our friends. Last spring I took from it a layered branch and started a new shrub. Now, at the end of May, it covers a circular area two feet in diameter. It is a mass of fresh leaves, with yet no sign of budding, while the parent plant is nearly in flower.

May I suggest one or two ways in which sage can be used in the kitchen? These may serve your culinary imagination as points of departure. You want roast potatoes with your steak or ribs or chops. Good! In a shallow baking pan pour enough olive oil to cover the bottom. Put the pan in a 400-degree oven. Throw into the hot oil a dozen leaves of sage and three cloves of crushed garlic. Remove both as soon as they are crisp brown. Peel medium-size potatoes, cut them in quarters, lay them in the hot oil, and sprinkle well with salt and pepper. Turn them as often as necessary to brown them on all sides. Poke with a fork and when done, put them on a paper towel, add more salt if necessary, and serve them forth. French fries are for teenagers to have with their milk shakes; potatoes done in this way are for adults of taste and educated palates.

In substantially the same way one may prepare lamb, pork, and veal chops. Remove from them every shred of fat. Sprinkle them with salt and pepper, place two leaves of sage on each, stack them in a bowl, and put them in the refrigerator for twelve to twenty-four hours. Then cook them in olive oil seasoned with sage and garlic as for the potatoes. Use very little oil, just enough to grease the bottom of the skillet. Add to it a bit of butter. When the chops are done, pour over them the juice of half a lemon and an ounce of white wine or dry vermouth, increase the heat, shake the skillet vigorously for about thirty seconds. Remove the chops to a heated serving tray, pour over them all the sauce that is in the skillet, and bring them to the table. If you want to feast the eyes as well as the palate, arrange the chops prettily and sprinkle them lightly with well-minced parsley.

And that brings us to the absolutely indispensable herb. If you should ask me to name a dish that a bit of parsley would fail to improve, I might be startled as by an impertinence. What do you mean "fail to improve"? What sauce, soup, or salad, what stew or omelet is not made better by the addition of fresh minced parsley? "How about custard pie?" you say. Well, I'm not so sure. Have you ever tried it *without* minced parsley?

Yes, indeed, any accomplished cook would agree that parsley has a much wider range of uses than any other herb. Angelina and Marcellina might rank it above garlic. For them, as for me, it would be one of those happy choices one does not have to make. There is always an abundance of both.

Parsley, as I have already noted, is the grand patriarch of a whole family of herbs: the *Umbelliferae,* the parsley family. It is a biennial that produces leaves in the first growing season and a flowering stalk in the second. There are two main varieties: the light green curly leaved, and the dark green flat leaved. The latter is often called Italian parsley. It is a very leafy plant, more aromatic than the other, and therefore the better of the two for culinary purposes. The other, very curly and light green, is frequently used as a garnish. However, when brought in fresh from the garden, it is not so inferior to the other as to make it a *poor* substi-- tute.

Propagation of parsley is by seed, and the plant is quite hardy. Germination is slow but certain, for parsley seeds are unusually viable. The plant grows well enough in ordinary soil and does not need a great deal of sun. However, in fertile soil, well watered and well drained, the plant achieves a Garden-of-Eden luxuriance. A row of such parsley, of the

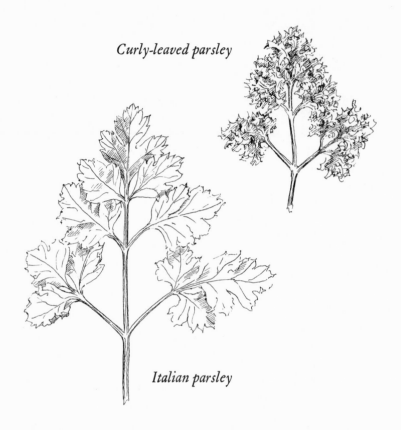

Curly-leaved parsley

Italian parsley

Italian variety especially, with the many-branched plants more than a foot high and the leaves a clean, deep, glossy green, pleases the eye as much as any ornamental shrub.

Once established in fairly good soil, a bed of parsley may be made permanent by self-propagation in any climate where the sting of winter is not deadly. Put the seed in the ground in the late fall or very early spring. After germination, when the plants are about an inch long, thin them so that they are three or four inches apart. During the first season the growth will be luxuriant. The leaves may be freely cut, and new ones will grow rapidly. A dozen plants will provide parsley for an entire neighborhood.

In the winter the growth is less vigorous, but the leaves remain green and the plant survives freezing weather as low as 18 above zero. In the second spring the plant burgeons once more and the fresh new leaves soon give way to the flowering stalk, which grows to a height of three feet. It produces many lateral branches, and at the end of each a seed pod will develop.

When a choice plant in the row begins to develop the flowering stalk, take up the whole plant and move it to wherever you want your parsley bed for the next season. In taking up the plant, make sure that you don't disturb the roots. Water it well a few hours before you move it so that the soil will cling to the roots. Dig deep with the shovel and take up plenty of soil, for the plant must not be aware that it is being moved. Set it in a hole prepared for it, firm the soil around it, water it, and leave it to complete its life cycle.

About the middle of June tiny greenish-yellow flower pods will appear at the end of the stalk and its many branches. The seeds will then form, mature, and fall to the ground in the late fall. And there they will lie through the winter. Very early in the spring they will germinate and the plants will begin to grow, slowly. By the time the leaves of last season's plants have given way to the flowering stalk, the leaves of the new plants will be ready for use. And you will never be without fresh parsley.

Parsley is usually planted in a circular bed instead of a row, but if you prefer the plants in a row, or placed here and there in your garden, they will transplant very easily when they are young, about two inches in length. Letting the parsley thus propagate itself, leaving the seeds to gravity, wind, and birds, you will discover new plants every season throughout the garden. Such has been my experience. I have never been so parsley-rich as now that I neither buy nor sow parsley seed.

There is, however, the ever-present possibility of bankruptcy; and I am aware of it and act accordingly. A few years ago the weather played one of its diabolical tricks; the temperature dropped to 10° F. early in November and I lost all my parsley. Since that disaster, I have potted a few plants every season and kept them out among the shrubbery, ready to be brought into shelter should the weatherman predict dire things to come.

In regions where winter always kills, anyone who wants fresh parsley on hand must use a flowerpot or windowbox. The parsley plant produces new leaves as the mature ones are cut away, so a few potted plants will provide a family's minimum parsley requirements. One thus unfortunately situated, who must practice strict economy in the use of parsley, should remember that parsley leaves grow from the inner core outward; in cutting leaves for use, always take the outer ones, snipping them with the shears or fingers at ground level, and leaving the new inner leaves to grow to maturity.

And what about the uses of parsley? They are too numerous to list. We used it finely minced last evening, together with Parmesan cheese and butter, on egg noodles. It flavored my scrambled eggs at breakfast this morning, and I shall scatter it on my bowl of chicken broth this evening for dinner. You take it from there. Give your imagination scope. Nor must you forget that if you tend to be scorbutic, a pot of parsley tea is the most pleasant of all antiscorbutics!

So much for the sage, parsley, and garlic that Angelina used in roasting fowl. The other two seasonings, celery and onion, are vegetables. I shall deal with them in Part Three.

Chervil, or beaked parsley, is an annual. It resembles

parsley and is propagated in the same way. Scatter the seeds early in the spring on a small patch of well-raked ground. Barely cover them with finely screened light soil or sand. Germination will be prompt. If the soil is fairly good and well tilled, you will have a healthy crop of chervil throughout the season.

Chervil

We are told that chervil is a native of Russia, that it was naturalized as a wild plant in our northeastern states, and that some people eat it as a wild potherb. We prefer to use it in sauces, egg dishes, salads, and in cooking fish. If you want a delicious light sauce for trout, combine a teaspoon of minced chervil, parsley, a clove of garlic, the juice of half a lemon, and two tablespoons of butter.

Tarragon is a perennial, and one immediately associates it

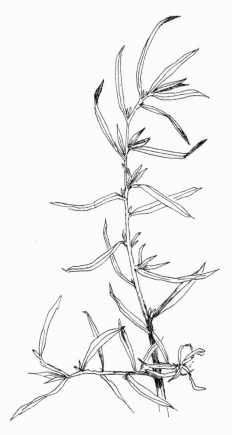

Tarragon

with vinegar. The plant is bushy, with many drooping, spidery branches and long, narrow, intensely green leaves a little larger than the leaves of rosemary. The root crown is matted and diffused. The new growth come up from it early in the spring. When full-grown, it reaches a height of two feet and requires a circular area about two feet in diameter. Propagation is by stem cuttings and root division. Procure a start from a nursery or seed store. The plant is hardy, but in extremely cold, subzero regions it must be protected in winter either by potting or heavy mulching.

Since tarragon is native to Russia, the Russians probably have many uses for it. We use it primarily in salads, to flavor wine vinegar, in fish sauces, and in cooking chicken. To flavor wine vinegar, fill a quart jar loosely with tarragon leaves, which have been washed and drained well, and pour into the jar as much wine vinegar as it will hold. Let it stand a week or ten days, then strain the vinegar and use it to flavor a full gallon.

There are two kinds of marjoram: the sweet or knotted, and the wild. The latter is also known as oregano. They are both perennials in temperate regions. Where the winters are severe, as in the northern states, they are cultivated as annuals. Of the two, the wild is the more hardy; it will survive near-zero temperatures. It also reseeds itself freely and may therefore survive as a virtual perennial even in very cold regions. Propagation of sweet marjoram is normally by seed. These are mixed with sand or very fine screened soil and scattered on carefully tilled, well-raked ground late in the spring. Wild marjoram may be propagated by cuttings and root division.

The two marjorams are very much alike to the casual observer. They attain a height of about two feet. The leaves of wild marjoram are rather coarse, hairy, and dark green; those of sweet marjoram are a lighter green and lightly downy. The flowers of both are pinkish white. The fragrance of the leaves and flowers of sweet marjoram is sweetish and lightly spicy; that of the wild is stronger, less subtle in its spiciness.

The culinary uses of both marjorams are considerable. They are used in meat sauces particularly, and in various stews. A salad will be the better for a few leaves of marjoram shredded into it. They are both used, but more particularly

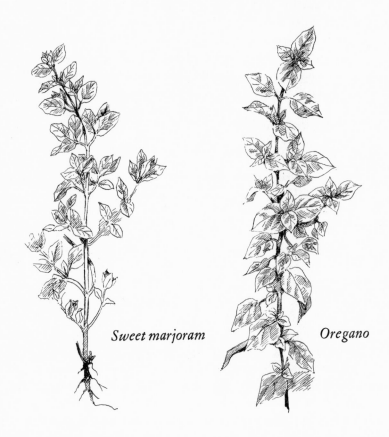

Sweet marjoram   *Oregano*

the wild, minced fine to season sliced tomatoes and cucumbers. Wild marjoram is the best herb for seasoning mushrooms. The Italians often call it *erba da funghi*, "herb for mushrooms."

There are half a dozen or more varieties of thyme, but *Thymus vulgaris*, garden thyme, is the recognized culinary leader of the family. It is a very hardy perennial, and if

Thyme

given some protection it can survive rather harsh winters. It is something of an evergreen, as it retains its leaves in the winter, like the sage, and sends forth fresh growth in the spring. So except in extremely cold regions, the fresh leaves are available all year round, but are most juicy and aromatic in the spring. They are very small, nearly round, about one-fifth inch in diameter, and a dusty green in color. The tiny abundant flowers are a very light purple.

Thyme grows in a tight, matted clump, a yard or so in diameter, nicely domed, with a considerable woody undergrowth when the plant is full-grown. The leaf-bearing stems on the matted woody undergrowth are rather short. In full resurgence in the spring, it is a very lovely plant. The bees agree. It likes lots of sun and a chalky soil, but it will do well in any ordinary garden soil.

Thyme can be propagated by seed, but the more successful way is by root division and layers. Like sage, when garden thyme is ten or so years old, the woody undergrowth becomes excessive. It should then be renewed. Take up an old plant early in the spring. Divide the root clump and replant those sections that have healthy, well-budded stems. Or take advantage of self-layering. (See p. 109 on layering techniques.) Where a low-growing stem touches the ground it develops roots at the point of contact with the soil. Investigate such stems, and where roots have developed, snip the stem midway between the rooted part and the parent plant. The detached portion will be your new plant. Set it wherever you like in your garden.

The culinary uses of thyme are numerous. Its peppery, mint-like flavor is pleasant but strong. Used in big doses, it will dominate a flavor instead of making it more subtle, more complex, more pleasant. Keeping this in mind, one may use thyme in all meat sauces, stews, vegetable and other heavy, hearty soups, stuffings, and in all types of pickling. It is particularly good for use in baking beans, provided one does not ruin the beans with too much molasses and tomatoes.

And one must remember, of course, that all these herbs—tarragon, the marjorams, chervil, thyme—can be used in combination with the better-known onion, garlic, chives, and parsley, in the making of stews, sauces, and stuffings.

Whether what they add is desirable or not one must discover for oneself.

So we are back in the kitchen experimenting, using our imagination, comparing notes with friends who share our interests, in the manner of my darlings, Angelina and Marcellina.

I remember Marcellina one evening in Angelina's kitchen, where we met so often, defending with her humorless passion *pasta al pesto* against Angelina's good-humored assertion that *pasta asciutta alla Toscana* was the best of all the pastas. The reader may perhaps know that the former is egg noodles, which the Italians call *tagliatelle* or *taglierini,* with a dressing of crushed fresh basil, garlic, butter, and grated cheese; *pasta asciutta* is any of the many forms of pasta with the classic spaghetti sauce.

They were quite a contrast, those two housewives! Angelina was stout, hearty in eating and drinking, playful and bawdy. Her round, shiny face reflected the fattiness of her kitchen. Marcellina was gaunt, precise, meticulous, proper, without conscious humor. I took delight in urging the one against the other and learning what I could about cuisine from their friendly banter.

"Holy Mother Mary, how time passes!" Marcellina said as she accepted a glass of wine. As usual, the talk was of gardening, cookery, and domestic economy. "Here we are at the beginning of April and we haven't made our garden yet. Have you put in your beans?"

"Yes," said Angelina. "My husband put them in this morning. Have you started your basil yet?"

"Not yet. We are waiting for the next moon."

"The next moon! What has the moon to do with it? You hill people do everything by the moon. You are so superstitious!"

"We may be hill people," said Marcellina, "but we understand gardening." Then, turning to me: "Ask Angelina who in the neighborhood has a better garden than mine. Ask her where she got her basil plants last year when her seed failed to germinate because she paid no attention to the moon."

Here they argued at length about the proper time to sow certain crops, the relevance of the moon, the causes of failure in germination. Wanting to bring both of them back to the lovely aromatics, I asked Marcellina which was her favorite.

"Basil," she said without hesitation. "It has a divine fragrance. None of the others smells as sweet and spicy. In our parts the men, especially the young when they go abroad with amorous intent, wear a sprig of basil behind the ear."

"Our young men need no basil to make them sweet and attractive," said Angelina. "We grow the herb to flavor tomato paste and minestrone." She was hankering for a little bawdy fun, but Marcellina would not rise to the bait.

"Basil was especially created for making *pasta al pesto*," Marcellina said. "There are a dozen sauces for pasta, but none equals the *pesto* made with fresh basil and garlic."

"Just a minute there! Not so fast! *Pesto* is very good, but it is not in the same class with the sauce we make for pasta in our region." Angelina turned to me for approval.

Determined not to be drawn into the controversy, I played it cool and managed an invitation to dinner from each of them. Angelina promised pasta with the classic sauce; and in sweet-basil time Marcellina would make for me *pasta al pesto*. Both would use home-made noodles.

One may well imagine that the dinner each served drew from me the highest praise. The truth of Marcellina's dictum that "herbs are the very soul of cookery" receives nowhere better confirmation than in these two ways of dressing pasta. What makes each a veritable culinary triumph is the fresh herbs. The essence of Marcellina's *pesto*, of course, is garlic and fresh basil reduced to a paste; and the "secret" of Angelina's classic spaghetti sauce is a combination of fresh herbs. Let me indicate the way she made it; then we shall proceed with our account of the indispensable dozen.

Ordinarily, the meat for sauce for six people is half a pound of round steak finely diced. If you are having chicken with the pasta, dice the liver, gizzard, heart, and neck and add to the beef. Cook the meat lightly in three tablespoons of olive oil in a saucepan; then add the following herbs minced: two cloves of garlic, four shallots, two tablespoons each of parsley and celery leaves, one of basil, and a teaspoon each of sage, rosemary, and thyme. After these, add a handful of dry mushrooms that have been soaked in boiling water and cut into small pieces. Simmer over a slow fire so that nothing browns, nothing burns. Add salt, pepper, a dash of allspice, a pinch of nutmeg. Mix well with a large spoon and moisten the whole with half a cup of dry vermouth or a good dry white wine. As the wine reduces, shake the pan and let the aromas find your nostrils. Then add a cup of tomato sauce, made preferably from your own tomatoes, diluted with half a cup of stock, or two cupfuls of whole ripe tomatoes lightly cooked. Simmer the whole for an hour if you used the sauce, or two hours if you used the whole tomatoes, fresh or canned. The finished sauce should be a rich burgundy brown with no trace of the tomato visible in it. The final ingredient, added a few minutes before the sauce is used, is two strips of lemon rind, finely minced. The lemon oil closes the aroma circle, and the sauce is done. *Viva la pasta asciutta!*

We now return to the garden, as we must, for a consistently fine cuisine requires frequent trips from the kitchen to the herb garden. We have yet to note the cultivation and use of several herbs among those I listed as indispensable in good cookery. I have already noted that all herbs do quite well in ordinary soil and with a minimum of care. Naturally, they all need some nourishment, and basil, native to the tropical regions of Asia and Africa, needs an abundance of heat. In the temperate zones, it is useless to plant it before the soil is warm and the sun has come to stay. Without warmth, it simply will not grow. In the Pacific Northwest I wait for Marcellina's moon to come around, about the middle of May. If when the moon comes, the weather is still cold and damp, I wait for the sun. Then I scatter the tiny, dark seeds in a seed flat in finely sifted soil and cover them with about a quarter-inch of sand and place the flat in the sun. When the seedlings are two inches or so long, I set them out ten inches apart and water them well. When the plants are rooted and well established, and summer is in full swing, they grow rapidly and need little care beyond regular watering.

Basil grows to a height of about eighteen inches. It has many branches and the leaves are large, so a dozen or so plants will provide as much basil as one is likely to use. It is in the nature of the plant to flower rather quickly; when the flowering stem develops, there is a consequent decrease in the production of leaves. Early fruition can be discouraged by nipping off the flower buds as soon as they appear. However, the basil plant will yield up its ghost to the first harsh frost of fall.

Basil may be used in other ways beyond making *pesto* and flavoring vegetable soups. Some like it in salads, in drinks, in sauces, in egg dishes. Minced fine, it is very good with sliced tomatoes. A boiling-water infusion may be made of the leaves, and the brew used as a carminative and a restorative to disordered nerves. We, however, exploit its preventive rather than its restorative virtues, using it mainly in the ways I have already suggested. *Tagliatelle al pesto* and minestrone soup flavored with minced basil keep us

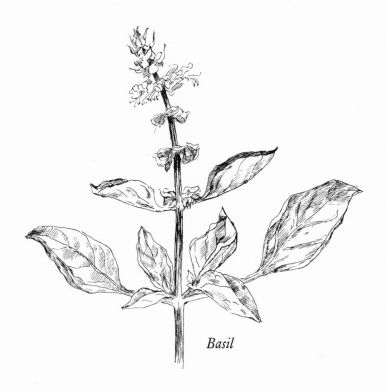

Basil

happy. Our nerves are thus in order and we have no need
for carminatives. We use it also to remind ourselves that
there is yet something in life that is sweet and spicy.

Devotees of *herbe royale* bemoan that its life is so brief.
Can it be extended? How can the leaves be preserved so
that one can have fresh basil throughout the year? When
dried and crumbled, it is to its fresh state as old age is to
youth—nothing but degeneration. Some have tried freezing
the fresh leaves; others have chopped them and preserved
them in olive oil. And one may, of course, as Angelina did,
use it to flavor that magnificent sun-dried tomato paste
conserva. We have tried all of these ways and found merit

in each one. Since we use basil primarily for flavoring vegetable soups and in making *pesto* for pasta, we preserve it by mincing it and mixing it with grated Parmesan cheese. This is the way to do it:

Wash a great quantity of basil leaves. Spread them on a cloth to dry in the sun for just a few minutes, until all the moisture from the washing has evaporated. Mince them very fine, until they are nearly reduced to a pulp, and put them in a large mixing bowl. Add grated Parmesan cheese and mix thoroughly. Continue adding cheese and mix until the cheese has absorbed all the liberated oil in the minced leaves. The final mixture should be as dry as sawdust. And here, a word of caution: the cheese must be a genuine, well-dried Parmesan. *Caveat emptor!*

To pack the mixture for preservation, first sterilize half-pint jars, as many as you need. Sprinkle a thin layer of salt and pepper in the bottom of each jar. Spoon in the mixture and press down with some convenient tool until you have a well-packed layer about a third of an inch thick. Sprinkle with more salt and pepper. Add another layer, another sprinkling of salt and pepper, and continue the process until the jar is filled to within a third of an inch from the top. Pour on the surface a quarter-inch layer of olive oil, screw on the cap, and store in the refrigerator. The sprinkling of salt and pepper and the abundant salt in the cheese are the preserving agents.

The method is completely effective. The end product is essentially a Parmesan cheese highly spiced with basil. It keeps well and for a long time. We are currently using a jar of it that was packed two years ago. There has been no perceptible deterioration.

It may be used in the following way: For one pound of noodles or other pasta, melt a quarter-pound of butter; add one heaping tablespoon of the basil-cheese concentrate, a clove or two of garlic finely minced, and two tablespoons of fresh minced parsley. Stir thoroughly until you have a smooth, flowing butter sauce. Pour it over the cooked and drained pasta and mix well, as you would a tossed salad. Add more grated Parmesan if you wish. Then eat heartily and wink at me if you like it.

Oh, you will like it well enough, and you will return to the garden with added zest, with renewed faith in the virtue that is yet in the spade and the hoe, even as I did.

Propagation on the land, and renewal of plants lest they degenerate with age is a type of horticultural insurance. In these ways the grower stays in business. But to the amateur gardener, to one such as myself who enjoys growing plants as much as eating what he grows, propagation tends to become an end in itself; and so, indeed, does the whole process of gardening. There is a special delight in observing the progress of propagation; in following the course of a plant's development day by day; in contemplating a healthy, well-nourished plant in soil properly cultivated and free of weeds. This morning when I looked at one of my young, layered rosemary plants, I was not thinking of an eventual harvest, or of the happy prospect, a year hence, of giving someone a start of low-growing rosemary. No, not at all. I was merely enjoying the phenomenon known as propagation.

Of all the methods of propagation, layering is the most fascinating, for it suggests the reproduction cycle of certain mammals. A low-growing branch of a shrub is pinned down with a forked stick where it is closest to the ground. Insemination and conception! Then follows the gestation period, the new plant taking nourishment from the mother plant while it is developing its own roots. To determine when this has been accomplished, scratch gently with the fingertips at the point where the branch touches the ground. If you see a

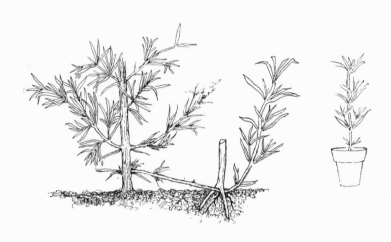

few thin roots, even no more than a quarter of an inch long, cut the branch well above the point where it was pinned to the ground. With the umbilical cord severed, the little plant is on its own!

In this happy way, by a symbolic act of primitive mating, I brought forth new plants of rosemary, *Rosmarinus officinalis*. Native to the Mediterranean coast, it is an evergreen and a fairly hardy perennial. It will survive temperatures down to around 15° F. Thus, in the extremely cold regions of the north it must be either potted or grown as an annual. It is a shrub with fairly large woody stems that resemble the grape vine. In temperate climates it will attain a height of four to six feet. Although the long narrow leaves endure through the winter and are good for use in the kitchen, it is the new spring growth that is best.

Rosemary is not at all fussy in its soil requirements, but it requires full sun. The plant may be propagated by seed, but germination is very slow. Propagation by root division, cuttings, or layering is the most effective.

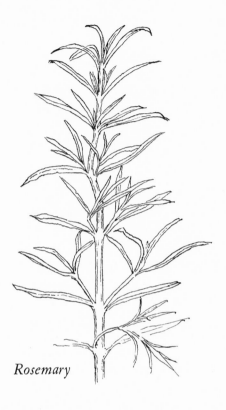

Rosemary

While we always had rosemary in the garden, and made full use of it, it was the Greeks, whom I first met in the flesh in an obscure little village at the edge of a forest in the Pacific Northwest, who made me vividly aware of its primacy as a culinary herb. Until then, I had simply taken it for granted as a plant my mother used in her excellent cuisine. All the Greeks had a plant or two in their vegetable gardens. One of them, the barrel-chested Gus, had a hedge of it. But it was their spectacular use of it that impressed me. And I now find myself wondering how we or they ever managed, in that damp region of giant conifers, to procure a start of rosemary. There must have been a will, and hence a way!

The Greeks celebrated Easter with a "paschal lamb" barbecue. I put it in quotes because what they roasted may have been a goat; I don't remember. What I do remember is that the animal was large and that their mode of preparing it for the table was utterly strange to me. They had made slits in the flesh into which they pressed bits of garlic and sprigs of rosemary. Thus prepared for roasting, the animal was spitted on a stout pole and turned by hand on a roasting spit over an open pit in Gus's backyard.

The men took turns keeping the carcass revolving over the fire; while two of them worked as turnspits, the others sang and danced, in the manner now made famous by Zorba the Greek, to the rhythm of their jolly native songs. The wine jug was passed from hand to hand; the sweat poured down their faces; the fat of the lamb dripped and sizzled on the coals; the air was charged with the appetizing fragrance of roasting, rosemaried meat. And I stood by, a young boy in a strange land, rapt in the wonder of marvelous plenty, following closely a new and exciting way of celebrating the Resurrection of the Lord. And learning, without being especially aware of it, that rosemary is the preordained herb in lamb cookery. I mean, of course, that for centuries the Mediterranean people have used it to enhance the flavor of sheep flesh. There are other ways, I'm sure, of preparing such meat for the table, but I urge you to try a leg of lamb in this way. Bone it and scatter in the cavity bits of rosemary and slices of garlic; salt and pepper it well and lave the flesh with olive oil and lemon juice; tie it firmly and roast it either on a spit or in the oven until it is done medium-rare. If you dislike blood-tinged meat, roast it longer. Then serve it with a bottle of red wine. Done in this way, it will provoke many a wink of approval. Treat lamb chops in the same way, then broil them; or trim away the fat and do them quickly in a skillet in olive oil.

And there are other culinary uses for the herb that grows so luxuriantly in the hills along the Mediterranean coast, and elsewhere in the temperate zone where there is some sun. It is an ingredient in many sauces along with parsley, sage, garlic, shallots. I remember that fresh, tender rosemary leaves were scattered on the surface of chestnut cake, a sweet I relished and ate so greedily when I was a child in Italy. And I remember that the minced leaves were worked into the dough of *panini,* the tiny loaves my mother usually made when she baked bread. Once rosemary is growing in the garden, the curious and resourceful cook will discover for himself the many ways in which it may be used.

In the inventory of my own garden I listed another herb, less familiar than rosemary, that deserves to be better known: English pennyroyal, *Mentha pulegium.* In Italy it is called *puleggio.*

Everyone knows how certain odors and tastes perceived in childhood, and then somehow lost, lodge in the memory and haunt one in later years. Occasionally, an odor perceived now, or a taste, or a particular flower, will recall that moment in the past when that odor or taste or flower made its first impression; and the experience is pleasant. But it is otherwise when one is haunted by the memory of something that was very pleasant on the palate, in the nostrils, or to the eye, and seeks in vain to recover it. The desire for its recovery may become very intense and the search for it relentless. The phenomenon, I suppose, occurs most often among people who were transplanted—as I was transplanted —from the Old to the New World.

In the world where I was born, there was, for example, a certain kind of apple. It was large and rust-colored. It was called simply *mela ruggine,* "rust apple." I liked it more than any apple I had ever tasted. Its fragrance, its taste, its size and color are in my memory, though half a century has passed since I last ate of it. I have sought its like in vain.

Shall I give up the search and live in the haunting memory of *mela ruggine?* Never! I shall return, some day, to Casabianca, where I was born, and my nose will lead me to the *mela ruggine tree....*

And there were frogs cooked in a sauce whose fragrance lived in my memory for years. Near Casabianca there was a swamp, a frog haven where now and then we caught a mess of frogs. Mother cooked them, the whole frog, in a tomato sauce and served them with polenta. Always with polenta. It was a dish that I liked with a passion. The herb that gave the sauce its delightful flavor and fragrance was *puleggio.* When we came to America we lost both the frogs and the herb. Neither was to be found in the Grays Harbor country. Frogs there may have been, for there were plenty of swamps, even one at our back door where we hunted snipe and caught plenty of them; but if there were frogs, they kept a safe distance from us. And of *puleggio* there wasn't a trace. However, the fragrance of frogs with *puleggio* remained vividly in my memory. It seemed strange that neither could be found. But I pressed the search. Surely, in a country so large, so rich and varied in resources, there must be, some-where, both frogs and *puleggio.*

And there were! I found the frogs first. When I had been in America twenty years I found them. On the way home from our honeymoon, an Italian section hand took us to a slough along the Columbia River. In the dark of the night, armed only with a railroad switchman's lantern, we picked them up mercilessly as they squatted on the stagnant water, transfixed by the strange light. We filled a sack and had a feast. But without *puleggio,* it wasn't the same dish at all.

Having found the frogs, I pressed my search for *puleggio*.
And I found it, at long last, in the North Beach section of
San Francisco. It was a small bunch, neatly tied, among
other cuttings of herbs in the vegetable bin of an Italian
grocery. "Put them in a glass of water," said the grocer. "In
two weeks the little sprigs will have roots."

I kept them in water in the hotel until I was ready to
leave; then I wrapped them in a damp cloth, tucked them
in my suitcase, and brought them home. The little sprigs

Pennyroyal or Puleggio

did root in water, and when I put them in the ground—it was in the fall—they began to grow almost immediately. I have not been without *puleggio* since.

As the name suggests, *Mentha pulegium* is of the mint family. It is a low, creeping plant that requires moist, rich soil and grows with weedy luxuriance. It is fairly hardy but will not endure severe winters. Since it reseeds itself so readily, this seems unimportant. In the spring new plants appear in the waste of the old. It is native to Europe, where its culinary value is much appreciated. There have been reports that it grows wild in California—probably introduced there by Italians.

The gardener may have difficulty procuring seeds for *Mentha pulegium*. An herb dealer may have them. If not, one should write to the herb gardener at one's state college.

We are told that the plant contains toxic oils; that it must be used in small amounts; that an infusion made from it is used in the treatment of cramps and spasms. It may well be. We use it extensively and with delightful results in all fish sauces, particularly those in which tomatoes are an ingredient, but in small amounts, not for fear of being poisoned but because only a little is required to produce the desirable results.

So we have an abundance of *puleggio*—but we have lost the frogs. They simply are not around in these parts. Dams on the Columbia have flooded my frog slough. But I shall press my search and find more frogs so that what has been so long in the memory may soon be on the menu. I will not give up until I have the quarry in hand. As I now have in hand the shallot for which I hunted so long in vain!

Perhaps you have heard of shallots. They are also called eschalots or scallions. But have you ever seen one? Do you know anyone who grows shallots in his garden? The answer is very likely no; for in America shallots live a very private

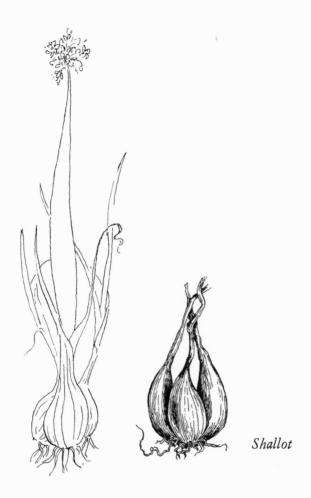

Shallot

life in French cookbooks. One finds them occasionally for sale on the East coast and in the more sophisticated food stores westward to the Pacific. In Seattle there is one market where one may see a tiny basket of shallots day after day, always in the same place, untouched, undisturbed, unwanted. The price is $3 a pound! Fortunately, shallots are not perishable. They live on and on and on and gradually wither away.

I began my hunt for shallots years ago. The greengrocers didn't have them; the nurserymen had never heard of them. They were not listed in the best seed catalog in America. I found them, at last, in the market mentioned above, three years ago. The price, then, was $2.44 a pound. I was a little startled when I saw the price tag and thought that a mistake had been made, so I checked with the clerk, who checked with the boss, who checked a price list, and I was assured that the price was correct. I was unconvinced, but they had me by the throat and I had to yield. Having searched for shallots for so long and having now found them I could not deprive myself simply because the price (more than three times that of garlic!) seemed to me outrageous. So I bought a pound.

With the shallots now in hand, I was reluctant to use them. I wanted to cook six pounds of tripe according to a recipe in which shallots were listed as one of the ingredients. The price of the tripe was 39 cents a pound. If I followed the recipe to the letter, I would need a little better than a pound of shallots for the six pounds of tripe. It seemed to me vulgar, decadent, even immoral, to pay $2.44 for one of the aromatics required to cook tripe worth $2.34. So I abandoned the project, temporarily.

Years ago I came across a recipe for pan-frying a sirloin steak. "Rub the skillet thoroughly with a quantity of shallots," had written the author, whose name I have forgotten. Surely he must have meant that a quantity of shallots should be sliced and sautéed in oil, and then the sirloin pan-fried in the aromatized oil. That would seem the more effective way of cooking the flavor of the shallots into the meat. With the shallots now in hand, that was what I proposed to do.

However, once again I could not, in good conscience, use

an aromatic whose cost per pound exceeded the cost of a pound of the finest cut of beef. So I abandoned that project, too, temporarily, and decided to plant the shallots in my garden. I would consider the purchase an investment and determine, by experiment, whether the shallots, so outrageously expensive, would grow in good soil in the Pacific Northwest.

And that was what I did. Every shallot I put into the ground yielded about three-quarters of a pound, so at harvest time one pound of shallots had increased to a bushel. The market value of the crop, I figured, was $75. In a few months an investment of $2.44 had earned $72.56! Holy Saint Christopher! I was about to rush to the phone and call the New York Stock Exchange and say, "Look fellows, you list blue chips, no? How about listing shallots, my shallots, that in four months have earned me such an astronomical sum that even I, a college professor, can't figure the percentage." But then I thought better of it. There were too many Uncle Harrys on the Exchange. They wouldn't understand.

Now bear in mind that up to this point I had not tasted the shallots. My sense of what is prudent had enjoined the use of a flavoring agent that cost as much as the meat it was to season. Now that I had such an abundance I was less reluctant to use them. So I did—and I became suspicious. Were these actually *eschalots,* those miracles of flavor without which there would be no such thing as the *haute cuisine* of France? I didn't think so. An aromatic that was so expensive must be difficult to cultivate. It must require a special soil, a special environment, the coaxing hand of a professional. If not, how could one account for the outrageous price? And yet in my own garden, they had grown so well! Was it possible that what I had been sold as shallots were in fact small onions? The palate was convinced that

I had been deceived. I consulted an herbalist, noted his description of the shallot, and then read: "Other kinds of onions are often sold as shallots."

So I had been taken! But I would have my revenge. I would learn for certain whether I had a bushel of shallots or a bushel of "other kinds of onions." I would press my investigation. I returned to the supermarket where I had bought them and interviewed the man in charge of the produce department. Did he know where the shallots were grown? No. Did he know where they came from? No. They were sent to him by the central purchasing department with instructions to sell them at a certain price. He thought they might have come from California. Did he know whether they were difficult to raise? No. Did he know why they were so expensive? No. Convinced that he knew less about shallots than I, I left him and pursued my investigation elsewhere: in Paris.

In no other cuisine does the shallot figure so prominently as in the French; therefore, the authentic shallot must be cultivated in France. And since Paris is the gastronomic center of France, the best, the authentic shallots must be available in Paris. Thus I reasoned. With the aid of a French scholar living in France, I set out to find the most reputable seed dealer in Paris. We found him: Vilmorin-Andrieux, at 4 Quai de la Mégisserie. And from him I bought forty-five seed shallots: *Bulbes à Planter, Échalote Poire, Première Sélection du Monde.*

They came to me at the end of March. They were considerably different in form and flavor from the ones I had bought at the supermarket. I put them in the ground immediately. By the end of July they were ready to harvest. The crop was magnificent. Looking at them as they were drying in the sun, one who knew not whence the seed bulbs came might very well have concluded that my little patch of land was their native habitat. And yet a good 7,000 miles separated the land in which the mother bulbs were grown from the land in which they had reproduced their kind.

I put 40 bulbs in the ground. The ratio of reproduction was about 8 to 1; so I harvested 320 shallots. Putting 120 aside for use in the kitchen, I planted 200 and harvested 1,600 the following season. Their market value—the price had gone up to $2.89 a pound—was close to $500. Once more I thought of phoning the Exchange. And I thought also of abandoning the university and going in for shallots: the American affiliate of Vilmorin-Andrieux de Paris. Better than plastics! I was tempted. But the prospect of making so much dough frightened me.

So I retained my amateur standing and found all my reward in the certainty that I had the genuine shallot, *Allium ascalonicum.* I have them now in such abundance that I can eat a dish of shallots with every meal and invite my neighbors to do the same.

The shallot is thought to have come originally from Syria, and it grows wild in Asia. It grows to a height of twelve to fifteen inches and is cultivated in the same way as garlic. The individual bulb that I procured at Vilmorin was egg-shaped and about an inch and a half long. The skin was brownish tinged with purple. Planted late in the fall or early in the spring, in ordinary garden soil, each bulb produces a cluster of five to ten shallots. These are harvested when the tops begin to droop and wither, in late July or early August. After they are dried in a mild sun for a few days, they may be stored for months in a cool, ventilated place.

In using shallots for seasoning one must remember that the shallot is related to the onion and the garlic. Accordingly, a few of them minced will improve the flavor of stews and nearly all meat and fish sauces. Green salads, too, are given bite and a more appetizing taste by the addition of several shallots finely minced.

PART THREE

Of Herbaceous Edibles

Vegetables for Late Spring and Early Summer Harvest

We are now ready to enter the vegetable kingdom, a world of edibles so varied, so lovely to behold, so inviting to the feast that the dedicated gardener may be pardoned for the understanding smile he bestows upon the strict vegetarian. There is merit, as we shall see, in a meal composed mostly of vegetables.

Shall we begin with a definition? A vegetable is any herbaceous plant, annual, biennial, or perennial, whose fruits, seeds, roots, tubers, bulbs, stems, leaves, or flower parts are used as food. A herbaceous plant is any seed plant whose stem withers away to the ground after each season's growth; this distinguishes it from a shrub or a tree, whose wood stem lives on from year to year. When the herbaceous plant is biennial, its life span is two years, and it usually produces seeds and flowers the second year; when it is a perennial, it has a life cycle of more than two years. Every spring, for an indefinite number of years, it resurges from an enduring root crown. An annual, of course, completes its cycle in one year.

In every region of the vegetable kingdom, there is an

attractive variety of herbaceous plants, of vegetables, that the land can be made to produce for the table. Naturally, the extent of the variety is not the same for all regions, but the variety is there to be discovered and enjoyed. There are root vegetables and leaf vegetables. There is a group of vegetables known as legumes. There are vegetables that grow on vines. There is not one but a whole family of cabbages. Botanists and horticulturalists have developed varieties of nearly every vegetable known. It is your privilege and mine to learn to know these vegetables, to grow them in our own gardens and enjoy them at our tables.

Given this attractive variety of herbaceous edibles, which of them, how many of them, shall you raise? Since you cannot possibly raise them all—unless you have space enough and live in a region where *all* vegetables thrive— you must choose. I suggest that you concentrate on those that you and your family like best. Beyond this subjective factor in the choice, there is another determinant you must accept: wherever you are, the climate of your region, the length of the growing season, and the time of the last frost in the spring and the first freeze in the fall, will determine what you may grow, when you shall put down seed, and when you shall attend to certain other procedures necessary to fruitful gardening. Therefore, the home gardener shall acquaint himself with the weather data of his region. If you have lived in your area for some time, you know its climate in a general way; if you want specific data you may have it for the asking from the local station of the U.S. Weather Bureau. Or write to the U.S. Department of Agriculture, Washington, D.C., and ask for Home Garden Bulletin No. 9. It will be sent gratis, a very useful publication, for it contains not only detailed weather data for every region in the country, but also other information useful to the home gardener.

However, one need not abide by such weather data too strictly, for there are ways of coaxing nature to accommodate to one's requirements. And these the home gardener will learn as he adds to his horticultural experience. He will be told, for example, that the production of artichokes in America is limited to certain cool, coastal counties of California; and that is a fact so far as the *commercial* production of that fine vegetable is concerned. But it is also a fact that a satisfactory crop of artichokes for home consumption can be raised in most states. The same is true of many other herbaceous plants that are technically regional. The home gardener must be an ingenious, persistent experimenter if he would enlarge the range of edibles he is able to grow for his own table. In his quest for a better life through working with the soil and growing good things for the table, I shall be his happy guide and offer him the benefit of my experience, as I have done in Parts One and Two of this book.

In this chapter I propose to write about those vegetables that are sown early in the spring and harvested in late spring and early summer. But before we get down to peas and carrots, there are certain useful preliminaries that we may profitably note. We have already considered in Chapter 2 the size of a home garden and its best location on one's property. Once this is established, the next thing to consider is how the garden area may be kept in production as much of the year as possible.

The inexperienced gardener, thinking of gardening as a spring and summer activity, is likely to conclude that when those seasons have passed gardening is at an end. Not necessarily so! The productive span of your garden, the number of months when you may sow and reap, will depend on the length of your region's growing season. In the extreme North, where the period between the spring thaw and the following winter's deadly freeze is relatively short, gardening is pretty much limited to the summer season, but in the South one may grow many vegetables practically the entire year. All along the Pacific coast west of the Cascades, where rain is abundant and winters are generally mild, one may grow certain crops most of the year, whereas in the hot, arid lands, where water is scarce and the summer heat deadly, one may garden effectively only so long as the accumulated moisture of winter and early spring remains in the ground.

Where you live, then, will dictate in large measure how you may use your garden patch most profitably. But that is not the whole story. Herbaceous plants differ in their sensitivity to cold and heat, and in any regional growing season there are more or less fixed periods of cool, warm, and hot weather. The experienced gardener will prolong the productivity of his garden patch by taking advantage of these facts of nature. He will sow in succession those crops that do well in cool, warm, and hot weather. Thus he will have some vegetables growing in his garden during the entire growing season of his region.

In achieving this end he will be guided by what we have learned in years of horticultural experience. There is no guesswork, no leaving the outcome of one's efforts to chance. We know which vegetables are very cold-hardy and which are moderately cold-hardy. We know the groups that require hot weather and those that thrive in weather that is moderately warm. Knowing these facts, we shall proceed accordingly and thus keep our garden area in production as much of the year as possible.

When spring is in the offing and one begins to plan his gardening venture, he is well advised to consult with his local nurseryman and seed dealer. These merchants are usually regional specialists in horticulture and deal in herbaceous plants that are adapted to their region. They are in continual contact with truck gardeners, and the practical information they thus acquire they will gladly pass on to the home gardener. They will know, for example, which varieties of a vegetable can be most successfully grown in the area. They may also have on hand, or help one to find, barnyard manures if one's soil requires organic nutrients.

Indispensable, too, to the home gardener who would explore fully what he may grow on his land are the catalogs of reputable seed growers. The best of these known to me is that of the W. Atlee Burpee Company, Seed Growers, Philadelphia, Pennsylvania 19132; Clinton, Iowa 52732; or Riverside, California 92502. The catalog is illustrated in color so that one may see how the plants look at maturity. And on every packet of seed are printed the appropriate instructions.

So much for useful preliminaries. We are now ready to get down to peas and carrots. I shall write first about a group of cold-hardy vegetables that may be planted early in the spring, four to six or even eight weeks before the average date of the final spring frost. This I shall follow with another group, not so cold-hardy, which may be planted somewhat later. These are vegetables that, where successive plantings are possible, will be brought to the table in late spring and early summer. In another chapter I shall deal with herbaceous plants that require warmth, and those that may be planted late in the summer for harvesting in the fall and early winter in regions where the garden can be kept in production for most or all of the year.

Group One.
Plant the Following Four to Six Weeks Before the Average Date of the Final Spring Frost.

ASPARAGUS. One of the very best and earliest of all spring vegetables, asparagus is always expensive. The reason that it costs so much more per pound than, let us say, cabbage, is that it requires two years from the time of planting to bring an asparagus bed into production, and then the yield per unit of land is relatively small. Since the plant is most at home in regions where the winters are cold enough to freeze the ground to a depth of several inches, its commercial cultivation is limited to the northern half of the country. This fact, however, need not concern the home gardener. Wherever you live, you may want to try your luck in raising asparagus. The advantage in the venture is that the plant is a perennial. Once the bed of asparagus is established, the yield, though relatively small per unit of land, will continue for decades.

So: Do you want to grow asparagus? Do you have the space? And the patience to wait for the second spring for your first harvest? If so, dig a trench about 15 inches deep, 18 inches wide, and 75 feet long; this will accommodate fifty-six plants spaced about 18 inches apart. Properly cultivated and given a yearly dressing of a complete fertilizer, the plants will yield enough asparagus, year after year, for a family of four or five.

Now back to the trench. When you are digging it, throw the excavated dirt on either side for later use. When the trench is dug, put in it a 4- or 5-inch layer of manure mixed with peat moss and rotted leaves or grass clippings. Cover that with a 3- or 4-inch layer of good soil and work into it about 8 pounds of a complete fertilizer. When this is done, secure from your nurseryman the Mary Washington or

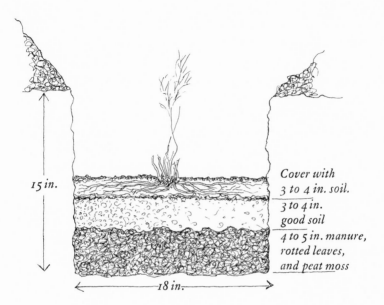

15 in.

Cover with
3 to 4 in. soil.

3 to 4 in.
good soil

4 to 5 in. manure,
rotted leaves,
and peat moss

18 in.

Waltham Washington variety of asparagus plants, one year old. Plant them 18 inches apart on the prepared topsoil in the trench, taking special pains to spread the roots of each plant to their full length, and more or less at right angles to the central root core or crown. Cover them with 3 inches of dirt. The trench will now be somewhat more than half filled and the unused soil will lie along its shoulders.

Here you may rest from your labor and have a cup of tea or glass of wine, and congratulate yourself on a job well done. Thus restored and at peace with yourself for having worked with such diligence and care, you may now go about your other garden tasks, keeping always an anxious eye on that asparagus bed. When, after more weeks than you thought you could wait, the little asparagus spears appear, delectable green upthrusts of about an inch, bring more soil into the trench and cover the spears nearly to their tip end. As they push their way upward to the sun, slowly, week after week, add more dirt to the trench and spread it evenly over its entire width, being careful to leave only the tip end of the asparagus spear exposed, until the trench is completely filled and level with the adjacent surface. Your asparagus bed will then be completed; the root crown of each plant will be covered with about seven or eight inches of soil.

Then, patience and restraint! Do not cut the first season's spears, for if you do, you may destroy them. The growth above the ground is necessary to the complete development of the plant root below. The second spring, too, you must master the eagerness to eat the fruit of your labor. The root crown is still developing and needs another season's growth above ground to achieve full maturity. Therefore, you may have but a taste of what you have grown. Cut only the larger spears as they rise above the ground during the first two or three weeks of the season. Thereafter, hold your knife! Let the spears come to full maturity and bear their seed. In the third spring, when the root of the plant is full-grown and well established in its deep bed of mulch and soil, you may gather the entire crop until early July. The spears that come thereafter will develop and go to seed. When, late in autumn, these wither and die, gather them and burn them or give them a deep burial.

In cutting asparagus spears for the table, remember that only the green, crisp, upper portion is edible; the lower, white part is woody and stringy. The asparagus spears sold at the supermarket are generally too long, and the lower half is total waste. Therefore, if the price per pound is 40 cents, the actual cost of an edible pound of asparagus is 80 cents. The home gardener will avoid such criminal waste, and bring to the table the finest asparagus, by cutting the spears at ground level when they are four to six inches long and densely green all the way. What a privilege to be so asparagus-rich—and the fortune got with joy in labor!

BROCCOLI. Known in Europe for centuries, broccoli came to the American table not many years ago. It is a member of the cabbage family and somewhat akin to cauliflower. The edible portion is the rather loose flower head on the plant's center stalk and the several sprouts that grow later in the axils of the leaves. The three best varieties are Di Cicco, Calabrese, and Waltham 29. A packet of seeds will yield better than 200 plants, which come to maturity in about three months. Like other members of the cabbage group, broccoli can be grown in most parts of the country where fertile, moist soil is at hand. The plant is cold-hardy, and also tolerates the heat of midsummer.

For the earliest possible harvest, sow the seeds in seed flats indoors as early as February. And here, a note on the use of seed flats: A seed flat is a box 4 inches deep and, normally, 12 inches wide and 24 inches long. One may construct a seed flat of whatever length and width suits his purpose, just so the depth is about 4 inches. The flat is filled with fine, screened soil and the seeds are placed in it, three or four to a group, each group spaced about an inch apart. When all the seeds are in place they are covered with about half an inch of sand or screened, loose soil and left to germinate. If the weather is very cold, the flat is kept indoors; if not so cold, the flat may be covered with a pane of glass and placed outside during the day. When the germination is effected indoors, and the plants are about two inches high, it is advisable, when the weather permits, to put the flat outside for the warmest part of the day. This gradual exposure accustoms the seedlings to the natural environment in which they must ultimately grow. One must watch the weather closely in early spring to avoid destruction of the tender plants by a severe cold.

Plants thus started in seed flats are normally transplanted to the garden when they are four or so inches tall. The transplanting procedure is normally followed in raising all plants of the cabbage family and some other herbaceous plants, such as celery. The procedure is a matter both of strategy and convenience. Where the growing season is short, and the time required for a plant to mature is long, one triumphs over time by germinating seeds in flats indoors, as described above. Where a plant that will bear transplanting is to be placed in a space in the garden presently occu-

Broccoli

pied by a plant soon to be harvested, time is gained by germinating the seeds in a small area and having the plants ready to be rooted when the space becomes available. And where gardening is done on a large scale, say where an acre or more of lettuce is to be set out, it is simply more convenient to start the plants in flats, or in a small area on the land itself, than laboriously to place each seed directly into the ground.

Back now to broccoli. Remembering that the plant is cold-hardy, and depending on the region in which you live, you may germinate in flats or sow the seed directly into the ground. The plant is large; it needs a space about 18 inches in diameter. If you are planting a single row, make a furrow about 2 inches deep and drop several seeds in spaces 18 inches apart. If you are using multiple rows, space them at 18 or so inches. Cover the seed lightly with soil and firm it down with your foot. When the little plants are 3 or 4 inches high, remove all but the sturdiest one from each space. Remove weeds as they appear, cultivate frequently, and hope for the best. Your job is done. If your soil is fertile and well manured, the plants will thrive. Otherwise, when they are 10 or so inches tall, scatter a handful of a complete, balanced fertilizer at the base of each plant.

The edible portion of the broccoli is actually the flower head. Cut the upper four inches of the flower cluster while the tiny seed pod is still green and tightly closed. When it begins to open and the yellow of the flower begins to show, the broccoli has passed its prime. You would be unkind to allow it to live so long. Nip it while it's still young and bring it to your table.

C A B B A G E . The most widely used and universally known of the cabbage group of herbaceous edibles is King Cabbage itself, the vegetable of the poor. There are reasons for this fact. The cabbage yield per unit of land surpasses that of any other vegetable. A fairly large head of cabbage, waste-free, will weigh about five pounds. The plant may be grown on a spot of land eighteen inches in diameter. To grow a like quantity of waste-free broccoli would require more than twice that land area, and four times that space is required to produce five pounds of waste-free asparagus. The economic consequence is obvious. On the current market, cabbage sells for 10 cents and broccoli for 20 cents a pound. The price of asparagus in season is 40 cents a pound. Thus, if cabbage is the vegetable of the poor, asparagus is that of the rich. But the poor have muscles and strong backs; and they can use those virtues to triumph over the affluent by growing their own vegetables.

There are other reasons for the abundance of cabbage and its relatively low cost. It can be easily grown at some time of the year in every state in the Union, and in many regions, the lower South, for example, and along the Pacific coast, one or more varieties can be grown throughout the year. While cabbage is ordinarily a cold-hardy plant grown early in the spring, horticulturalists have developed varieties of it that will tolerate heat and can therefore be grown in midseason and later. Certain vegetables, such as carrots and asparagus, require a certain kind of earth bed, but cabbage will grow on all soils that are fertile, moist, and of good texture. Fertility is important; the cabbage is a hulking peasant with a field hand's appetite!

There are several more or less standard varieties. For early spring planting, Golden Acre and Early Jersey Wakefield are the best; Globe and Copenhagen Market are midseason favorites. For later planting, the varieties recommended are Flat Dutch and Danish Ballhead. The home gardener should consult his nurseryman and seed merchant regarding the varieties best suited to his region.

How many varieties shall you grow? If one, which shall it be? Shall you germinate the seeds in flats or sow them directly outdoors? Or buy the few plants you need from the nursery? Each gardener must answer these questions according to his individual taste and requirements. A family of four or six hearty feeders is not likely to consume more than about twenty-five heads of cabbage a season. A packet of seeds will yield more than 200 plants, nearly half a ton of cabbage if the heads range in weight from four to five pounds, a rather moderate weight for a well-grown head of cabbage. So, how addicted to cabbage are you and the hungry mouths for whom you are responsible? Assay your needs and proceed accordingly.

For the earliest crop of cabbage, germinate the seeds in flats, as recommended for broccoli. Sow the seeds toward the middle of February; by late March the little plants will be ready to set out as soon as the ground can be worked. For midseason and later crops, sow the seeds directly into the ground. Whatever procedure you choose, remember that a single cabbage plant requires a circular space of approximately 18 inches. Plants should be set 18 inches apart; and where seed is sown directly in the ground, when the plants have formed their second set of leaves and are about 5 inches high, they should be thinned to that distance from each other. Thus, for twenty-five cabbages, reserve an area 1½ feet wide and 40 feet long.

Given all these considerations, a gardener who has limited space may want to buy the few cabbage plants he needs. If so, he will forego the pleasure, the considerable pleasure, I might say, of germinating his own seed. Oh, well! That loss he will soon forget as he weeds and cultivates his plants and gets caught up in the excitement of watching them respond to his skilled and solicitous care. At intervals of three or four weeks, once the plants are well rooted and growing apace, he will scatter at the base of each about a third of an ounce of some nitrogenous fertilizer that his nurseryman will recommend, and in less than three months from the time of planting he will take to his kitchen his first head of Early Jersey Wakefield cabbage. Three lusty cheers!

Or more than three and even lustier if the cabbage is sound, healthy, and prime for the table. And it will be so if the gardener protected the plant from the ravages of root maggot, caterpillar, and aphis, the three deadly enemies of the cabbage group, and cut it for the table at the proper time. To defang the maggot that destroys the cabbage root, one must treat the soil with an appropriate garden dust such as Diazinon. The various manufacturers of insecticides may not give their products against the same insect or plant disease the same name, so one had better inquire at the local garden store or nursery about effective insecticides, and then use them as directed by the manufacturer. I have found Diazinon dust effective against the maggot, and have occasionally used a nicotine spray known as Black Leaf Forty to destroy aphis and caterpillar. But these seldom appear in such numbers as to constitute a threat to my cabbages. The maggot, however, I have had to reckon with, and I have done so, mercilessly and effectively, with Diazinon. Identify the enemies of herbaceous edibles that plague your region, and proceed against them with the appropriate weapons.

Having done so, come harvest time, bring a sound head of cabbage, cut in its prime, to your kitchen. Cut in its prime! That means taken in its crisp, tender, juicy youth, that stage in its development when the discriminating eater will mutter between crackling bites, "O my lovely cabbage! Thou art the thing, the very thing itself!" And when he praises thus, he knows whereof he mutters.

When is a head of cabbage in its prime? What we call the head is actually, in cabbage structure, the seed pod of the cabbage in embryonic form, if I may put it a trifle loosely. Left alone, the head will eventually burst open at the apex, and from its center will rise a branched stem to a height of three or more feet, at the terminal end of which and on its several branches it will bear a multitude of pale-yellow cruciferous flowers, which in turn mature into seeds. The cabbage plant develops in two stages. First it forms a head, and all the nutrients the plant takes from the ground and the air are used in forming that head. When the head is completely formed, the flowering stem, an elongation of the cabbage stem itself, begins its growth toward complete maturity. The cabbage head is formed when, whatever its size, it is closed at the top and feels firm though somewhat resilient when pressed. The leaves around the head, curved gently inward, seeming to hold the head as in a vase, will be firm and their color clean. The cabbage is now in its prime. It will remain so, pretty much unchanged, for some time where the weather is cool. Later, depending on the degree of increase in the sun's heat, the flowering stem will begin to develop, the head will lose its color and begin to crack, the surrounding leaves will wilt and droop. The cabbage has had it! But before that happens, the informed gardener shall have had his cabbage and may want to give what remains to Peter Rabbit.

L E T T U C E . Of all ordinary cool-weather vegetables, lettuce is the most easily offended by heat. The soil in which it thrives is slightly alkaline and it must be prepared with care. Spade into it a commercial fertilizer rich in phosphorus in whatever amount per square foot is recommended by the manufacturer. Then level the area and rake it thoroughly until the soil is clean of stones and rubbish and is pulverized. It will then be ready to receive lettuce seed or seedling.

Since it is so sensitive to heat, lettuce can be grown in the southern latitudes only in the fall, winter, and spring. In northern regions one may grow it in the spring and fall. In the colder regions of the northern latitudes and in high-altitude areas, lettuce will do well in summer.

For the earliest harvest, it is advisable to germinate lettuce seeds in seed flats, sowing the seed at the very start of spring. Trace little rows in the soil two inches apart and about half an inch deep. Drop two or three seeds at one-inch intervals all along the row. Cover them with a quarter-inch layer of screened soil or sand and await germination. When the plants appear with a well-formed pair of leaves, thin them to an inch apart; when each plant has four or five leaves, transplant them in neat, straight rows a foot apart. Space the plants every ten or twelve inches. A packet of seeds will yield several hundred plants. Germination of lettuce seeds takes a relatively short time; most varieties mature in two to three months. Do not hesitate to set the plants out as early as you can; light frost will not harm them.

As the spring season advances, lettuce seeds may be sown directly into the ground, which many gardeners, including myself, prefer to do, without recourse to germination in seed flats. When this procedure is followed, thinning becomes a very important operation. I must therefore repeat here to emphasize what I said on this subject in Chapter 1. The seeds of lettuce, as of nearly all vegetables, are tiny, and one is tempted to put too many in a given space. When this is done, thinning becomes difficult and laborious. Therefore, proceed with patience and care, dropping the seeds sparingly in the furrow as suggested above for the seed-flat procedure. Even so, thinning will be necessary.

In all forms of horticulture, the purpose of thinning is to provide fruit, flower, or vegetable the amount of space it needs, both above and in the ground, for full development.

In thinning a row of vegetables, be guided by the following facts of horticulture: Plants differ in vitality. Some are genetically weak; others may fall prey to insects or disease. The ones that survive, like fruit on a tree, will not all mature at the same time. Furthermore, many annual vegetables achieve maturity rather quickly. If they are not harvested, they complete their life cycle and go to seed. In the flowering stage they are not desirable for the table.

For these several reasons it is desirable to do the thinning of certain vegetables in several stages. The spacing required for lettuce plants, for example, is about a foot. The first thinning operation is done as soon as the tiny plants are an inch or so long. Remove as many plants as is necessary to provide an initial spacing of an inch or so. When the plants have grown another inch, thin again, increasing the space

to four inches from plant to plant. And, of course, with each thinning remove the weaker plants and those damaged by insects or disease. A week or so after the second thinning, the surviving plants will be healthy, durable, and ready for the salad bowl. The plants removed in the succeeding thinning operations will be used in the kitchen.

When thus ready for use, though not yet full grown, the entire crop of lettuce cannot be gathered at one time. Nor would you want to. Go to the garden to take whatever you need for a given dinner until that planting is exhausted. Now that all the plants are healthy and growing well, you should harvest those that are nearest to full maturity, leaving the smaller ones to continue their growth. This selective harvesting is prudence, a means of enjoying as many plants as possible before they complete their life cycle. There will be more lettuce for the table; waste will be reduced to a minimum.

So much for the ways and rationale of thinning. Now some final remarks on lettuce. There are two types: head lettuce, and loose-leaf, or more simply, leaf lettuce. The first matures to a firm, solid head; the second, full grown, is a large rosette of leaves their color, size, and structure depending on the variety. One trims away the outer coarse leaves of head lettuce and eats the head; of leaf lettuce, one eats the leaves, there being no head. However, the center leaves of some varieties of leaf lettuce thicken into a cluster that may be regarded as an embryonic head.

There are several varieties of each type. Black-seeded Simpson, Grand Rapids, Oak Leaf, Saladbowl, and Slobolt are well-known varieties of leaf lettuce. The last two are the most tolerant of heat and are therefore recommended for late planting and general cultivation in the warmer zones. Of head lettuce, White Boston, Fulton, Great Lakes, and Iceberg are some of the better-known varieties. In your region there may be varieties not listed here. Once again, consult your local seed merchant and choose from such regional varieties as he may recommend.

In making your choice, if you have no strong preferences rooted in taste and experience, remember these facts: Leaf lettuce is richer in food value than head lettuce. It also has a more decided and characteristic flavor. Head lettuce tends to be watery and bland. Leaf lettuce, because it is green, its

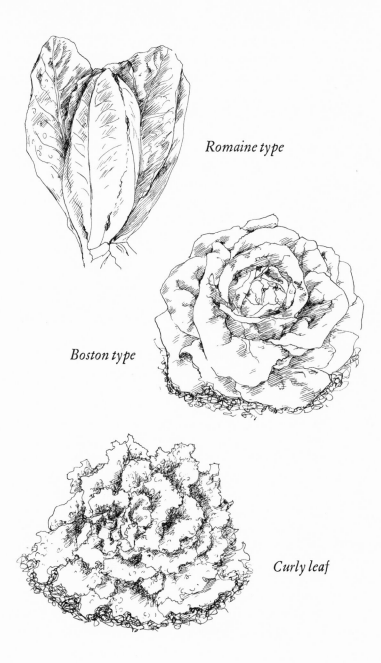

Romaine type

Boston type

Curly leaf

leaves rich in chlorophyl, is of that group of vegetables, most of them green-leaved, that have the highest content of vitamin A, plus significant traces of minerals and other vitamins. Head lettuce, like cabbage, because it is bleached, hasn't enough vitamin content to be worth recording. Nor does it have much flavor. It is easy to manage in the kitchen, however. It need not be washed, as does leaf lettuce. One merely slices it like bread and serves it with, likely, Thousand Island dressing. And that may well be the reason—and the fact that it is durable and ships well—why in America it is by far the most popular salad green.

Head lettuce should be harvested for the salad bowl when its head is about half formed. At that stage it will have most of the virtues of leaf lettuce. When fully mature, the head is firm, solid, like that of a cabbage, and the surrounding leaves will be aged, dull in color, blotchy, limpish. When it is half formed, or thereabouts, the head will be rather loose and the leaves will bend inward, folding one over the other to complete the structure of the head. The surrounding leaves, like those of a young cabbage, will be a healthy, clean green in color and firm in posture. Thus, head lettuce, in its early stages of development, green nearly to the core, will have both the gustatory and nutritious virtues of leaf lettuce. And this latter, too, is at its best when the plant is nearly mature and all its leaves, especially the outer ones, have the firm upthrust of youth. Their very appearance then will tempt one to bend to the ground and eat them in the manner of a blissful ruminant. To feel that temptation in all its earthy insistence, and to delight in it, may well be the true measure of a gardener whose dedication to horticulture is rooted in a continuing desire for good food.

ONIONS AND LEEKS. In joining these two I do homage to their affinity and affirm it. Both the onion and the leek, eaten raw—how else?—leave their essence for some time after they have been ingested, much to one's embarrassment in circles where an onion or leek breath is not socially acceptable. And for this very tenacity, raw onions and leeks are in ill repute. But not with me. I eat heartily of them, let the breath blow where it may!

Their affinity manifests itself in other ways. Wherever an onion will grow, in whatever soil or climate, so will a leek. They are both cold-hardy and tolerant of such summer heat as one is likely to get in the temperate regions. In the South they thrive in the fall, winter, and spring; in the North, in the spring, summer, and fall. Along the Pacific coast west of the Cascades, leeks sown in late spring will survive the winter unless it is abnormally harsh.

Both onions and leeks require a loose soil of moderate fertility. Both have a thick cluster of fine, hair-like roots; the soil must be loose for their effective penetration as they grow and probe for nutrients. Five pounds of a complete horticultural fertilizer to each hundred square feet, scattered evenly and worked into the soil with a rake, will supply the necessary fertility for onions and leeks.

One may start onions from sets, seedlings, or seed. Sets are tiny dry onions. They are put in the ground early in the spring and covered with about an inch of soil. A three-inch space between the plants is adequate. Sets are especially recommended for the production of spring onions, also known as green onions or, more loosely, as scallions. Seedlings are small onion plants, available, as are the sets, at the seed store. Firmed into the ground early in the spring, spaced the same as sets, they will produce green onions in a few weeks. The ones that are not harvested as spring onions can be left to mature and taken up later for storage as dry onions. The tops of the remaining plants should be bent at the base and lodged when they are full grown. The proper time to do this is when the green tops begin to turn yellow and lose their vitality. With the top bent and lodged, all the plant's energy goes into the bulb, the onion itself, to its greater glory.

If you are not in a hurry, there is considerable merit in starting onions from seed. Germination is very slow. Seeds put into the ground at the earliest possible time in the spring will produce fully mature onions in about four months. The harvest, however, may begin late in the spring, when the onion is at the green-onion stage. Thereafter, as you thin, in accordance with the procedure outlined in the paragraphs on lettuce, you can bring the onions to the kitchen in various stages of development. The ones not thus harvested will remain in the soil and achieve full maturity.

Leeks are normally grown from seed, and they may be advantageously transplanted. I recommend this procedure. Put seed directly in the ground as early in the spring as the land can be worked. Germination will be very slow. Have patience. When the plants are 5 or 6 inches high, transplant them 4 inches apart in a straight, shallow trench about 3 inches deep. The reason for setting them in a trench is this: The leek is structured somewhat like a green onion. The edible part is the lower, round, white section, which may reach a diameter of nearly two inches. To procure the largest possible edible section, leeks are "hilled." That is, soil is banked up around them in successive stages as the plants develop toward maturity; in this way, since what is underground will be blanched, the length of the white portion is increased. Leeks in good soil, properly hilled, may have a white portion as long as seven or eight inches. The function of the trench is to facilitate the hilling of the plants. That's all. One merely adds soil to the trench; when the trench is filled, the leek is fully hilled.

Where winter temperatures do not drop lower than six

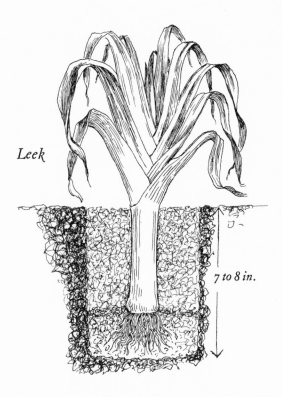

Leek

7 to 8 in.

or eight degrees below freezing, leeks sown in May may be transplanted at the end of June or early in July and left in the ground for harvest through fall, winter, and early the following spring. Early, I say, because as the spring season advances, the seed-bearing stem of the leek, in the form of a hard, woody kernel at the leek's center, begins to develop and the leek becomes progressively undesirable for eating. A leek well on the way to seed maturity can be better used to club a man than to tempt him.

In leeks, there is no virtue in mere size. A well-cultivated leek the diameter of one's finger, its leaves green and erect with only a slight curvature at the tip, is just right for eating, especially when it is eaten raw, dipped in a piquant mixture of olive oil, lemon juice, salt, and pepper. What an accompaniment to broiled lamb chops and fine bread, the thought thereof nearly maddens me with hunger. So I must hold my pen and strike another vein.

Of onions there are more than a dozen varieties; of leeks, but one. Fittingly so! The one and only leek! The pride of Wales!

Yellow Bermuda and Granex are large, flat-ended, mild onions of short storage life, particularly adapted to the South. Onions that store moderately well and are recommended for temperate regions are Golden Beauty, Fiesta, Bronze, Perfection, and Sweet Spanish. In the Northeast and Midwest one may grow Southport White Globe, Southport Yellow Globe, Ebenezer, Early Yellow Globe, and Yellow Globe Danvers. These varieties store well. For northern regions, a hybrid known as Early Harvest is recommended.

PEAS. He who has not eaten green peas directly from the vine, shelled and popped into the mouth, must not, for sweet charity's sake, be told what he has missed! Have you had them so, tepid with the late June sun, green, crisp, tender, juicy, sweet with that special vegetable sweetness that is sweet-not-sweet? If not, bestir yourself and beget peas on your patch of ground and bless me for having goaded you into so much goodness.

Bless me! For you shall have no reason to curse me, as Mike once did, when he discovered the embarrassment I had caused him. Mike was a fellow worker in the sewer ditch where I labored one summer between school terms, the better to provide for a growing family. As dessert to his lunch, Mike always brought a bag of fresh peas and ate them out of the shell, boasting that, by a strategy he refused to divulge, he produced more peas per pod than any other grower, amateur or professional. Driven to theft by my passion for peas, I stole into his garden and ate my fill. Beginning at one end of the row, I worked my way leisurely to the other, shelling and eating peas and leaving the empty pods on the vine.

Some time later Mike went to his garden with a neighbor lady on whom, so it was rumored, he had amorous designs. Intent on winning the lady with peas—less wholesome means have been used to achieve amorous ends!—he walked with her to the pea row, she with her basket and he with his passion, filling her ears with chatter about his well-filled pea pods.

Imagine the rest! My pilfering was discovered and I was roundly cursed. But I had had my fill of peas. You may have yours without curses, a twenty-five-foot double row of peas for the price of a packet of seeds and a bit of labor. Or do you want twice that many?

Peas and the spring season go together like two peas in a pod. Decidedly a cool-weather crop, pea seeds should be sown as early as possible in the spring. In the lower South they are grown in the spring, autumn, and winter. In latitudes above the lower South they are grown in the spring and the fall. In the northern states and at high altitudes, they can be grown in the spring and summer. However, no matter what the region, the early spring crop is the best. And the home gardener may simply want to let it go at that.

When the ground is ready, trace two shallow furrows a few inches apart, as long as you desire. Place the pea seeds in them, one seed every two inches, and cover them with an inch of fine, loose soil. When the plants are a foot high, bank a little soil around them, working carefully with a small hoe so as not to injure the roots. Some pea vines grow to a height of five or six feet. These should be given support. If tree branches of that length are available, stick them into

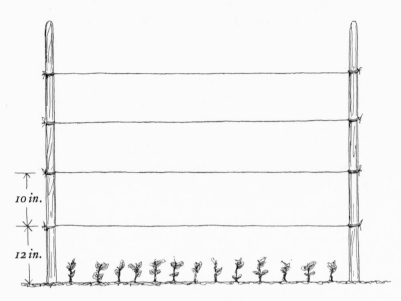

10 in.

12 in.

Peas—supported by twine between two poles

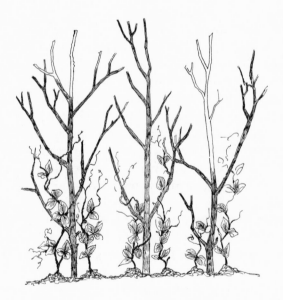

Peas—supported by branches

the ground between the furrows of the double row, at intervals of about a foot. If you have several double rows, space them about every thirty inches. Where branches are not available, sink a sturdy pole at the end of each row between the two furrows and run lengths of heavy twine from pole to pole, beginning a foot from the ground and on up at intervals of ten inches. Germination, if the weather is right, is fairly rapid. In three to four weeks the vines will be on their way up, their curling tendrils circling branch or twine.

Green peas are prime for the table when the pod is fully formed, smooth and green. Press it between thumb and forefinger to determine if the pea inside is formed. Full, rounded swelling of the pod is not a certain indication that the pea is ready for harvest, so the visual test must be checked with the tactile. When I pilfered Mike's peas, not wanting to shell in vain, I tested each pod with my fingers, a trick I had learned from Mike himself. Just a touch of irony and a bit of prudence!

And here, a little reminder: remember the weeding, watering, and cultivating instructions outlined in Chapter 1. And fertilizing, too. Unless a fertilizer of other composition is specified, a bit of a complete, balanced fertilizer applied at the rate of five pounds per hundred square feet will pay dividends in raising nearly all vegetables. It may be worked into the soil before planting or scattered around plants when they are well started.

POTATOES. I doubt that any home gardener can raise better potatoes than he can buy at a good supermarket. Quality potatoes can be raised only in soil of considerable acidity, soil of which the *p*H factor is slightly below 5. And that is a higher degree of acidity than is found in most garden soils. One may add sour mulch to the soil to increase its acidity, but it may not be worth while. Furthermore, a potato that is taken directly from the garden to the kitchen is in no way superior to one that has been in storage for weeks or even months. Unlike peas and certain other vegetables that are best when they are harvested young, the potato is prime for the table when it is completely mature. As a matter of fact, when the potato vine has completed its life cycle and lies wilted on the ground, the potato itself may be left in its bed of earth for some time without impairment to its quality. When I was a young lad and first turned the sod of America's prodigal land with my father, we dug up the mature potatoes as we needed them until it was convenient to take them all up. The soil provided good storage.

All these factors taken into account, then, and since considerable space is required to grow a family's supply of potatoes, the home gardener whose plot of land is small may want to buy his potatoes and devote all his land to vegetables that he can raise more profitably. However, a dish of potatoes is a very fine dish, and you may want to grow your own just for the fun of doing so and for the excitement in digging up a hill of six beautifully formed baking potatoes such as the state of Idaho may boast of. If so, here is what you should know:

Since the potato is a cool-season crop, it will not thrive in the summer in the South, or anywhere where summer heat is intense. The soil, as for the growth of all root vegetables, should be light and fertile. If your soil is not very rich, add a balanced garden fertilizer at the rate of ten pounds for every hundred-foot row. (In Chapter 2 I discussed the potato's space requirements.) Prepare the land in the fall so that it will be ready for seeding as soon as you can get to it in the spring. Rake the fertilizer deep into the soil a week or ten days before the potato seed is put into the ground.

The potato seed is a section of the potato itself. All potatoes, and especially the ones certified for seeding, have what are called "eyes." These are little dimples whence, eventually, the potato vine grows. For planting potatoes, cut a medium-size one of certified stock into blocks, each one of which must have at least one eye, but not more than two.

Block of potato

Dig a furrow 8 inches deep, set the potato seeds in it eye up, spaced about 18 inches apart, and cover them with 6 inches of soil. In three weeks or so the potato plant will appear.

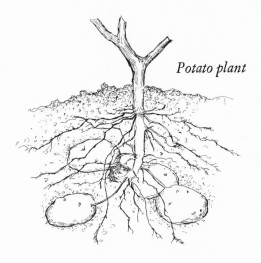

Potato plant

When it is well established and about 10 inches high, bank each plant with about 2 inches of soil. Each seed will produce about six large potatoes. As they grow toward maturity they may outcrop above the ground. When this happens cover them with an inch or so of soil; for such exposure to the light makes the potato green and unfit for the table.

The potato requires at least four months to mature. Planted

in late February, where possible, or early March, it can be harvested toward the end of June. As the spring season advances and rainfall decreases, irrigate your potatoes frequently. They require a lot of water.

One who is determined to raise his own potatoes may as well cultivate some for early summer use and others for storage. Irish Cobbler is a fine variety for early use. Katahdin and Russet Burbank are the best varieties for storing for winter use. There are several regional varieties, too. Inquire at your seed merchant's about varieties best suited to your area.

Have you ever baked a prime potato in the primitive way? I mean one of those oblong, unblemished beauties with a rather earthy, rough skin that are mealy and almost granular when baked. Have you ever baked such a prize tuber in a heap of hot ashes and coals, the remains of a huge fire, and eaten it hot, crackling skin and all, with just a bit of salt and a trace of ash to make the primitive feast authentic? A word to the wise—but you know the rest!

SPINACH AND TURNIPS. These are the two last in the group of vegetables that can be sown as early as eight weeks before the average date of the final spring frost. I shall deal with the turnip in a later chapter, listing it among exotic and less familiar vegetables.

Spinach is very hardy and will endure winters in the South. In the northern latitudes it is grown successfully only in the early spring and late fall. Where summer temperatures are mild, as along the Pacific coast, it may be grown from early spring until late fall. It will do well in any soil that is fertile, well drained, and slightly alkaline. Four pounds of a balanced fertilizer for each hundred square feet, worked into the soil before sowing, will supply the necessary fertility. Unless you are certain that your soil is on the alkaline side, work a bit of lime into it along with the fertilizer.

Drop the seeds an inch apart in shallow furrows and cover them with about half an inch of soil. When the seedlings appear, thin them according to the directions given earlier in this chapter, removing enough of them to provide a 5-inch space between plants. One packet of seeds will be enough for a 30-foot row. Rows should be 15 to 20 inches apart.

When the warm weather sets in, spinach tends to shoot up rather quickly, and when the plant is in flower, its quality is somewhat impaired. To assure a continuous harvest of prime spinach before the hot weather comes, seed the rows at intervals of two weeks. When the plants show signs of budding, and it becomes necessary to harvest more than one needs at the time, the surplus can be frozen for later use. I shall have something to say in the Epilogue about freezing vegetables.

Virginia is a variety that matures in less than two months. Bloomsdale Long Standing is the most popular variety. It is very productive, requires somewhat longer to mature than the Virginia, and will endure more heat before bolting. Virginia Savoy and Hybrid No. 7 are best for fall planting in regions where the growing season extends into the fall and early winter.

Group Two.
Plant the Following Two to Four Weeks
Before the Final Spring Frost.

BEETS AND CARROTS. These two root vegetables are pretty much alike in their soil requirements, except that the beet is more sensitive to acidity. The difference in this respect, however, is so slight that where the one thrives the other can also be expected to do well. What is extremely important for both is soil structure. Heavy soils with so much clay that they tend to harden when dry are not for beets and carrots; no amount of fertility will compensate for the blockiness of such soil. All root vegetables, and particularly those that are long-rooted, such as the carrot and the parsnip, require a loose, light, sandy soil. As the root, the edible portion of the plant, develops in length and rotundity, it needs room for expansion; the soil must give way to it. Light soils yield; heavy soils resist. The consequence of resistance is carrot roots that are prongy, gnarled, and rough. A carrot grown in the proper soil will be smooth and free of any lateral root fibers. Moisture, good drainage, and ordinary fertility are the other soil requirements of both beet and carrot.

In the southern latitudes, where the heat of summer is intense, the carrot is cultivated in the fall, winter, and spring. In the North, where winters are deadly, it is grown in the spring and through the summer. Along the Pacific coast, it may be grown in the spring, summer, and fall.

Carrot seeds are tiny; germination is slow; the mature plants need no more than half an inch of space between them. Thus, of carrots that are about an inch in diameter, one may grow eight to ten per foot. Drop the seeds carefully in shallow furrows, putting down two every inch along the way. Cover them with half an inch of very fine, screened soil. When the plants are a couple inches long, thin them to half an inch apart. Care in seeding will lessen the labor of thinning. One packet of seeds is enough for a forty-foot row. Successive sowings three weeks apart will ensure one a continuous supply of prime carrots; but this pleasure is reserved for those who live in regions where the growing season is longer than a single season. Chantenay, Nantes, and Imperator are the standard carrot varieties.

Fairly tolerant of both heat and cold, beets can be grown anywhere in the country. Naturally, a deadly freeze will do the beet no good; so in the northern regions where winters are extremely severe, beets can be grown only in the spring, summer, and fall. Where summers are very hot, the germinating seed will require constant moisture.

Beet seeds are larger than carrot seeds, and they germinate more quickly. What appears to be a seed is actually a little crinkled ball, about the size of a match head, which contains several seeds. Thus, in each little ball dropped into the ground, there are inherent several possibilities of germination. It is well to keep this in mind while sowing the seed. Beet plants should be spaced three inches apart, in rows somewhat more than a foot apart. Thus if you put down one of those little brown balls every three inches along the row, you will be certain of at least one germination and the labor of thinning will be reduced to a minimum. One packet of seeds is enough for a thirty-foot row. Seeds should be covered with an inch of screened soil, and whatever thinning is necessary should be done when the plants are two inches long, well established, and recognizable. You will know them from weeds by the reddish color of the stem.

If you enjoy the tops of beets, the so-called beet greens, do the thinning in stages. The first may be done when the plants are about six inches long and the beet itself only just beginning to form. And these will be brought to the kitchen, for which the gardener will be enthusiastically applauded, especially by children who are compelled, as they ought to be in any sensible family, to eat green vegetables. The succeeding thinnings will be done when the beet is in various stages of development; then the children will be privileged to eat beets and beet greens together. Thanks, my darling daddy!

Beets, like carrots, may be sown at three-week intervals to ensure an ample supply when they are prime for the table. When are they at their best? Not necessarily when they are small and very young. Nearly all root vegetables, as they grow to complete their life cycle, first develop the fruit itself, the root; then they put forth the flowering stem.

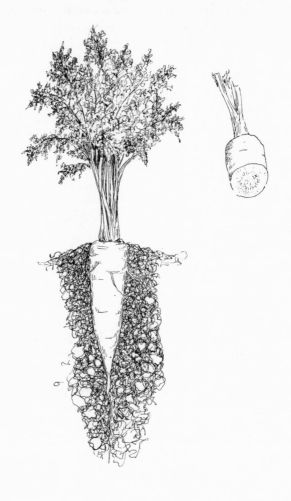

When the one stage of development is completed, the other begins. This, of course, is only relatively true. In the same sense that when one is born one begins to die, the development of the fruit and the development of the flowering stem may be said to begin at the same time.

However, the relative truth here is decisive over the absolute truth. The flowering stem of the carrot, the beet, the turnip, is at the center of the root fruit. It is there, could one but see it, when the root begins to form. But while the plant is growing toward maturity, everything it takes from the soil and the air is manufactured into nourishment for the root fruit until that has grown to its normal size; thereafter, the plant begins to nourish the flowering stem and continues to do so until the seeds are ripe. Until this phase of development sets in, the carrot, the beet, the turnip will be crisp and tender throughout, but as the flowering stem at the center begins to develop, it increases in circumference and becomes increasingly woody. As the evolution of seed unto seed progresses, there will be less and less of the root fruit that is edible. And what little there is will not be very good. Cut down the center a young but mature carrot, and one that is old. The first will be carroty all the way to the center; the other will be mostly kernel-pale, woody, tasteless.

The one stage of development does not end and the other begin simultaneously. The one progresses imperceptibly into the other. Once a carrot is mature, tender and crisp and carroty to the center, it will remain so for some time, longer if the weather does not get too hot. Its leaves will be sturdy, erect, a dense green in color, with no sign of yellowing. The mature beet will have sound, erect leaves, a deep burgundy in color, and none of them in process of wilting or decaying. A mature carrot bent in the middle will break in two pieces with a sharp crack. At such a stage, these root vegetables are prime for the table.

This is not to say, of course, that very young beets, carrots, and turnips are not good when they are quite young, half or less their normal size. They are very good in their infancy and ought to be eaten if they are available. It is doubtful, however, that they are as good as when they are fully mature; and it is certain that they are not better. The sensible procedure for the gardener is to eat some when they are young, and catch the others at maturity. And if he wants the undiluted flavor of the carrot, let him pull one out of the ground, rub off the soil with his hands, and, with feet planted firmly on his patch of ground, crunch it in the sun of spring.

CAULIFLOWER. The word means, literally, the flower of the cabbage; and the cauliflower is, indeed, a variety of cabbage. There is even a suggestion in the name that it is the cabbage of the refined, the rich. This may have been more true once than it is now, for the relative difficulty of growing it made it more scarce on the market than cabbage. It is still more expensive than cabbage because the yield of cauliflower per unit of land is less than that of cabbage. A head of cabbage may weigh six, even as much as eight or ten pounds, whereas a cauliflower, though the plant requires the same land area as the cabbage plant, seldom weighs more than three or four pounds. Nevertheless, cauliflower is abundant and, when in season, well within the means of ordinary mortals.

Cauliflower is a little more fussy than ordinary cabbage in its life requirements, but the home gardener who works with care will have his flower of cabbage. Hardy it is, but it will abide less frost than cabbage, and too much heat will prevent it from heading. Thus, in the South it can be grown in the fall, winter, and spring; in the North, in the spring and fall. In areas of high altitude it can be grown throughout the summer. It is adapted to any type of land that is fertile and well drained.

The life span of a cauliflower plant is the same as that of a cabbage. The plant requires about four months to produce a mature head. In the North, the plants for a late spring and early summer harvest should be set out as early as possible. It is therefore advisable to buy what plants you need or sow the seeds in seed flats late in February or early March. The procedure in starting plants from seed is the same as for cabbage. A packet of seeds will yield more than a hundred plants. For a fall harvest, the seed can be sown directly into the ground in June so that the plant will come to maturity and form a head when the cool weather comes. In the South, where cauliflower culture is possible in all seasons except summer, there is no need to start the plants in seed flats.

Rows of cauliflower should be spaced about two and a half feet apart; each plant needs a circular space of approximately twenty inches. Snowball and Purple Head are standard varieties. Treat the soil against root maggot as for cabbage (see page 138); counter caterpillars and aphis infestation with an effective spray.

The edible part of the cauliflower is called the curd. It is an aggregate of stems and flower buds tightly clustered in a convex mass. The structure is so tight that it is often difficult to fragment a head of cauliflower. If it is loose, with visible space between the buds, the head is either imperfect or is past its prime. The size of a mature head will vary; it may be anywhere from four to ten inches in diameter. But size is largely irrelevant to quality; compactness and purity of color, a clean white, except in the purple variety, are a better indication, as is the state of the plant itself. When the head is fully formed and mature, the encircling inner leaves will be virile, a clean green, and curved gracefully inward over the head. Catch it at that stage and enjoy it before degen-

Blanching cauliflower

eration in leaves and head begins.

The heat and light of the sun injures the cauliflower head. When the head is about half its normal size, gather the leaves over it and tie them into a protecting hood.

R A D I S H E S . These crisp, watery, pungent nuggets, round or cylindrical, red or white or particolored, so refreshing when eaten chilled and pleasant to bite into, are erroneously thought to have negligible food value. They have, in fact, a fair amount of vitamins and minerals. And they are easy to grow on any type of fertile soil. Their sensitivity to cold and heat is like that of the cauliflower. They grow quickly and pass their prime quickly. A packet of seeds scattered over an area six feet square will yield edible spring radishes in four or five weeks; and in another week or ten days a family will have crunched joyously the entire crop. Hence the advisability of repeated sowings at frequent intervals. Rake the soil thoroughly, scatter the seed, work it in with gentle taps of the rake's prongs, spray the soil with water, and the work is done.

Scarlet Globe, French Breakfast, and Cincinnati Market are spring varieties that mature in a few weeks. China Rose and Long Black Spanish are winter varieties that require about three months to mature. These should be planted in the late summer so that they will be mature in the fall.

P A R S N I P S . Parsnips require warmth but do not like midsummer heat. Hence they are grown in early spring in the South and in other regions where summers are excessively hot. Along the Pacific coast they can be grown both in the spring and in the fall. The fall crop, left in the ground during the winter, will actually improve in freezing weather that is not too severe.

Since the parsnip, like the carrot, is a long root vegetable, it requires a soil that is loose and light to a considerable depth. Heavy clay soils resist normal development of the root. Germination is slow. Put seed in the ground in shallow furrows two feet apart. Drop a seed or two every inch along the way. Firm the soil over it, cover it with a layer of peat moss, and keep it moist. This will aid germination. When the seedlings are two inches long, remove as many as necessary to provide two inches of space between the plants. One packet of seeds will yield several dozen plants.

As already suggested, the mature parsnip left in the ground does not soon degenerate. If the fall crop survives the winter, it will be in excellent condition for the table during the early weeks of spring.

One final reminder: herbaceous edibles must eat. When spading the garden plot, work barnyard manure into it if that is available, and always, a week or so before planting, rake into the soil about five pounds of a complete fertilizer for every hundred square feet. The effort and expense will pay dividends. Where other kinds of plant nutrients are needed, I will specify them. Good luck!

Vegetables for Late Summer, Fall, and Later

We are now ready to consider a second main group of vegetables, those that are sensitive to cold and must not be planted until the danger of frost is past and the sun has taken the winter's chill out of the earth. But before we proceed with these, we'll pause for a moment to survey what we have done as it relates to what we have yet to do. I assume that you have worked along with me and done all that I have suggested. If you have, then we have accomplished a great deal, my esteemed partner in pleasant and fruitful labor! So let us relax for a moment, pull the cork on a good bottle, sit in the gentle sun of spring, and rejoice in our achievements. We have rooted in the earth a goodly number of herbaceous edibles, thirteen to be exact. These are approximately a third of the total number that I shall urge you to grow with me to the greater glory of our leisure hours and our dinner tables. Only a third, but a substantial beginning! We raise our glasses to work well done. Be of good cheer. There is much more to do.

Look back with me for just a moment. Except along the

outer rim of the entire Pacific coast and in the lower South, the dates of the final killing frost of spring range from April 10 to the end of May. Only in a few isolated areas, such as northern Maine, central Idaho, and west-central Wyoming, does the danger of frost remain until the end of June. This means that the vast majority of us began our horticultural activities some time before April 10 or May 30, since we got our cold-hardy plants into the ground six weeks before the date of the last killing frost of spring. We were at work on our plot of land in late February, March, or April, depending on where we live. It was still cold and in many places wet, and we waited for fair days to get onto the land. We are now at the threshold of the frost-free season, whether early May or early June, a time for planting those vegetables that are not cold-hardy. What do we see as we go to the garden, tools in hand, ready to undertake the second phase of our enterprise?

We see, first of all, a variety of growing plants, a section of our garden plot in complete production. The plants we bedded in the earth weeks ago are in various stages of development toward maturity. Some of us, weather-lucky, have already harvested radishes, lettuce, and spinach, plants that mature in two months or less. We see the root of the beet beginning to thicken into a ball; carrots thinned and well on their way; cabbage and broccoli taking on their definitive forms. The pea vines are well up and in full bloom. How lovely the whole! What promise of pleasure at the table! Once more we lift our glasses. Then we roll up our sleeves, take hold of the rake and the hoe, and go to work. We must get our bean seed into the ground. We rake the area that had been spaded earlier, and otherwise prepare the soil; as we firm the seeds into the ground, we keep an eye on the pea vines. When the beans begin to entwine around the supporting poles, we shall be eating peas; and

when the pea harvest is over, we shall be having our first
beans. And then? Oh, there will be more . . .

Group One.
Plant the Following Vegetables on the Frost-Free Date.

B E A N S . Before we take up the cultivation of the bean,
we'll note an important attribute of the plant itself. The
bean is a legume, and the name derives from *Leguminosae,*
the name of the botanical family to which it belongs. Other
well-known members of the family are peas, lentils, chick-
peas, fava beans, vetch, and alfalfa. These vegetables have
attributes in common: they are rich in a protein substance
called legumin, and they are soil-improvement crops.

Beans enrich the soil by taking nitrogen from the air and
transmitting it to the soil through the agency of nitrogen-
fixing bacteria that are massed in globules along the plant's
roots. Since nitrogen is a principal plant nutrient, some of
these vegetables, especially vetch, alfalfa, and field peas, are
grown by the astute farmer primarily as soil-improvement
crops. Accordingly, it is wise to plant beans and peas in a
different section of the garden each season. In this way a
continuous supply of nitrogen is taken from the air and
distributed throughout the soil.

It is unfortunate that the bean itself, the dry bean, is
regarded as the food of the poor and as prison fare, and
has no status among the respectable, for beans are both
very nutritious and very tasty when properly prepared for
the table. Dry beans are rich in both proteins and minerals;
they are used a great deal in the cuisine of the French,
Italians, and Spanish. Cassoulet, a fine, savory stew of beans
and various meats, is highly esteemed, and properly so, in
certain parts of France. Green beans, of course, are a very
respectable food, rich in minerals and vitamins, and it is

with these that we are principally concerned in this chapter. Principally: for I shall also have something to say about the green-shell variety.

What immediately impresses one about the bean group is the variety. Beans of which the immature pod is eaten are called snap or green beans. Some have yellow pods and are called wax beans. The ones that grow on a vine that entwines around a supporting pole are called pole beans. Those that grow on a low, shrub-like plant are called bush beans; these may be green-podded or yellow. There are green-shell beans, shelled for the table as one does peas. There are bush and pole lima beans, large-seeded and small. The soybean and the fava bean are very good but not widely used. And for each one of these types there are several varieties. If one could harvest each variety of each kind, each in its prime, and put them all on display, the spectacle would please the eye and make the mouth water. I refer my fellow gardener to a seed catalog such as Burpee's, ask him to survey the varieties, and then decide how many he can grow on his land.

Happily, the bean, no matter the variety, can be grown at some time or other anywhere in America. It will do well in average garden soil of normal fertility and adequate drainage. Where the soil is rather heavy and tends to bake in the sun, thus making it difficult for the seedlings to break through the crust, it is advisable at sowing time to cover the seeds with a fine, loose, screened soil mixed with peat moss. Once the seedlings have broken ground, the roots will make their way well enough through the heavy soil.

It is futile to put bean seeds in the ground before it has been warmed by the spring sun. In the lower South and Southwest, green beans can be grown in the fall, winter, and spring; they will not do well in extremely hot summers.

In other regions, where the last frost of spring comes in April or May, and the first in the fall comes in September or October, the profitable growing season for beans is limited to the four or five months between those dates. If the weather is with him all the way, the gardener may provide himself with a continuous supply of prime beans for the entire season by successive sowings at two- or three-week intervals.

The procedure for growing the several varieties of green and green-shell beans is pretty much the same. For the bush variety, trace a straight furrow about 4 inches deep. Drop one seed in it every 2 inches. One packet of seeds will be enough for a 25-foot row. If you plant two or more rows, space the rows about 2 feet apart. Cover the seeds with an inch of soil and press it down with your foot. This firming of the soil aids germination. When the seeds have germinated and the plants are 3 to 4 inches long, do whatever thinning is necessary to provide a space of 4 inches between plants. When the plants are well established and a foot high, bank a little soil around them with the hoe, being careful not to destroy the roots by cutting too deeply or with too much zest. This banking of the soil is actually a form of cultivation: it destroys weeds, aerates the soil, and prevents too-rapid evaporation of moisture. The healthy, green plants will appreciate such husbandry; you will see them nod approval.

Pole green beans need a supporting pole and more room than the bush variety. Trace the furrows 30 inches apart. Drive an 8- or 10-foot pole, about the diameter of a broomstick, firmly into the ground every 30 inches along the row. Distribute six seeds around the pole, 3 inches away from it, and firm them into the soil as directed above. When the plants are 2 or 3 inches long, remove all but three or four to each pole. It will pain you, I know, as it does me, who

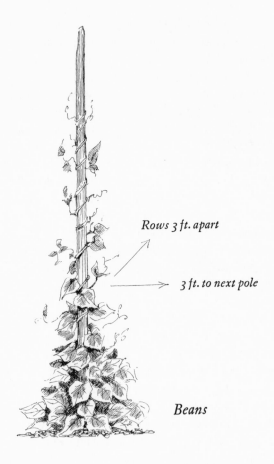

Rows 3 ft. apart

3 ft. to next pole

Beans

should by now be inured to that sort of distress, to uproot and destroy that which is good; but you must steel yourself to the task and take it on faith from me, your compassionate guide, that more than three, at the most four, bean vines cannot inhabit one pole. And that's that!

The above procedure is effective in cultivating all varieties of pole and bush beans. An alternate way of providing support for pole beans, and the one used by commercial growers, is as follows: Set substantial posts well into the ground at both ends of the bean row. Stretch two wires between the posts, one at the top and one at the bottom. When this is done, and you have made sure the wires are taut, run a length of stout twine from the top to the bottom wire at intervals of twelve inches. As the bean vine grows, its groping tendrils will find the twine. The rest is all a lively climb.

Just a note, now, on limas and soybeans. These require warmer weather than other beans and should be planted two weeks later. Both require hot weather and four months to mature. It may therefore be inadvisable to try to grow these beans in northern New England and the northern parts of other states along the Canadian border. However, if you have lots of space and can afford to risk a failure, I would urge you to try. It's so immensely satisfying to triumph over nature! You are more likely to succeed with Clark's Bush, Thorogreen, and North, three varieties of the bush lima. These mature more quickly than the pole variety. Bansei and Giant Green are widely grown varieties of soybeans, but the gardener had better learn from his seed dealer which variety is most likely to do well in his region. For regions where the lima bean is thoroughly at home, the recommended varieties are Jackson Wonder, Henderson Bush, King of the Garden, Challenger, and Fordhook 212.

Of snap or green beans, bush and pole, the following are among the best varieties: Pencil Pod Wax, Kinghorn Wax, Burpee's Brittle Wax, all yellow-pod bush beans; Topcrop, Bountiful, Improved Tendergreen, green-pod varieties. Of the pole type there are more than a dozen varieties. These are among the most popular: Kentucky Wonder, Blue Lake, Burpee's Golden, and McCaslan. Horticultural, Dwarf Horticultural, and Romano are the finest beans of the green-shell variety.

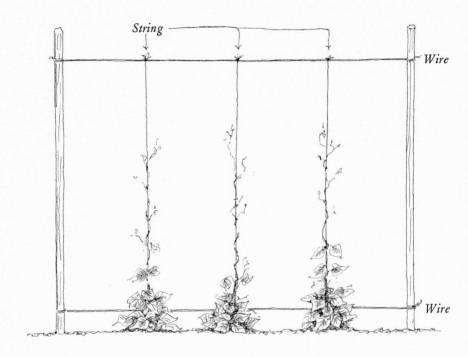

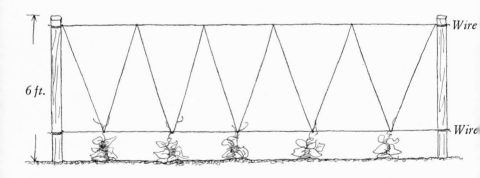

Supporting beans

All beans here noted require from two and a half to three months to begin to produce pods mature enough for the table. Much depends on the weather. A variety such as Blue Lake, which, theoretically, should mature in sixty days, may temporize and try the anxious gardener's patience if the season does not become progressively warmer from the date of sowing. If the weather remains cold and damp after the seed is bedded in the soil, it may be necessary to sow the seed a second time. Bean seeds that do not germinate in two weeks may have rotted. Remember these possibilities and proceed accordingly.

The mature pod of green beans varies in length from five to nine inches, depending on the variety. The pod of the bush type is generally somewhat shorter than that of the pole. Some pods are flat; others are round. They also vary in color, though most of them are green. Read the descriptions of each variety that are printed on the seed packet and in the seed catalog so that you may know what to expect and when to begin the harvest.

So that you may proceed wisely and enjoy the finest fruit of your labor, this is what you ought to know: The life cycle of the bean is, of course, from seed in the ground to seed in the pod. The development is, roughly, in two stages: first, the pod grows to its normal size, then the bean within the pod develops to maturity. Thereafter, if left on the vine, the pod changes color, shrinks, withers, and becomes brittle-dry. The bean within, too, shrinks somewhat, dehydrates, and hardens. In that stage it is harvested, shelled, left in the sun for a few days, and stored for later use as any ordinary dry bean.

What we want, however, is the green pod, not the dry bean. When shall we take it from the vine? Of all green vegetables the green bean is surely among the most esteemed. Of ten people taken at random, some may not like spinach;

all will enjoy the green bean. We look anxiously for its appearance at the supermarket, and pay dearly for the first crop of the season. We want it fresh, crisp, tender, grassy, for that is when the green bean is at its best. And since it is rarely available in all its pristine goodness, we who are wise and have a bit of land grow it ourselves.

When shall we take it from bush or vine? The pod is ready for the pot when it has grown to a little better than half its normal size. Some would insist that at this stage, in its virtual infancy, the pod is in its absolute prime for eating. They may be right, though I doubt it, and shan't quarrel with them. It is indubitably good, but I have concluded, after years of the closest intimacy with green beans, that though the pod may not improve as it grows to its normal size, its quality is certainly not impaired. This being so, it would be foolish waste to harvest all green beans when the pod is only half its mature size. The wise procedure is to begin the harvest when the pod is young and continue to harvest selectively, taking always those pods that are nearest to normal size.

And there are visual and tactile tests for determining when green beans are prime for the table. Whatever its length, a pod that is firm, solid, smooth, of true color, green or yellow or whatever shade is appropriate to it, will be excellent. Grasp it with thumb and forefinger, bend it at the middle, and it will snap cleanly in two. Furthermore, the bean inside will be either embryonic or so small as to be inconsequential. As soon as shell degeneracy sets in, that is, when the vine's energy goes to maturing the bean inside, the pod begins to lose color, shape, and crispness. When it approaches that stage, one may as well let it progress to seed maturity.

In order for a bean plant, vine or bush, to produce a continuous supply of prime pods during its entire productive life, it must grow and develop at a normal pace. In part, such growth will depend on the weather; for the rest, the gardener must assume the responsibility. Hence the importance of cultivation and fertilization. When the weather is as warm as the bean plant requires and the gardener's work is well done, there will be fine green beans for the table. Otherwise, the bean plant will be a retarded member of the herbaceous community—and offspring of retarded parents are to be pitied, not devoured.

And now a word about green-shell beans. If you like shell beans, or if you would learn to like them, then you must get a packet of seeds and grow some in your garden. It is far and away the most savory member of the entire group of legumes. And don't doubt my word! Sprinkle no ice on my enthusiasm for fresh shell beans! I shall have a dish of them for my dinner this evening with broiled Italian sausage!

The best of the named varieties is the Romani. Its requirements and cultivation are the same as for any other bean. The fruit we want of the Romani vine, however, is the mature bean, not the pod, although the pod itself may be taken in its prime and enjoyed like that of any other green bean. In fact, certain fine restaurants take pride in serving their guests green beans of the Romano variety. In some markets they are sold frozen as Italian green beans. But we shall grow them primarily for the mature bean.

The Romani is ready for the table when the pod, having achieved its full maturity and bulged with total pregnancy and changed color from green to light brown, begins to wither slightly. But only slightly! It will have lost its drum-tight compactness, will feel limber and pliant to the touch, but the shell itself will still be rather green in texture, though not in color, and moist, not in the least dry. At that stage, the bean inside is large, mealy, succulent. As the shell loses its moisture and begins to dry, the bean undergoes the same change and becomes less desirable. Gather the pods before that happens. Are you itching to harvest the first crop? And to use Romani shell beans in your next cassoulet? Good! Proceed! And good luck!

EGGPLANT AND OKRA. To pass from green beans to eggplant and okra is to go from the national to the regional in herbaceous plants. Whereas all people know and like green beans, relatively few know okra and eggplant; and not all who know them like them. They have a textural quality that offends some people: when cooked they are somewhat slimy.

I have eaten eggplant, now and then, prepared in a variety of ways, since I was a child, and it has always failed to excite me. The first time I had okra was thirty years ago in Lake Charles, Louisiana. It was a conspicuous ingredient in chicken gumbo, one of the best soups I have ever had. Eating it was a memorable gastronomic experience. I attributed the excellence of the soup, its unique quality, to okra. I have tried soups of the same name in many other places, but the similarity between what I had had in Lake Charles and the others did not extend beyond the name. I wrote to the chef at the Lake Charles restaurant and asked for the recipe. It was sent promptly; and though it was written in what appeared to be English, I could not derive from it anything intelligible. Either the chef or his secretary must have been somewhat short of literate. And so I have come to terms with fate and resigned myself to enjoying the memory of that chicken gumbo, the particular excellence of which must have been due to okra. Thus, even though okra is not produced in the latitude where I live and is not often seen at the market, when I do see it I always think of that chef in Lake Charles and wish that he had been as effective in communication as he was in the kitchen. That he intentionally garbled the recipe in order to preserve a culinary secret I have steadfastly refused to believe.

No such experience relates me intimately to eggplant, but I can become a little excited over it on purely aesthetic grounds. The fruiting plant is a lovely sight. The fruit itself, especially the Burpee Hybrid, a large, smooth, glossy, dark-purple ovoid, tucked at its stem end in a calyx of pale green and hanging against a background of large, serrated, pale green leaves, has a rare floral beauty.

For these several reasons, and for the further reason that they are both warm-weather plants, I have grouped them together. Of the two, eggplant requires consistently warmer weather and a longer time to mature. Plants for both should be started in seed flats two months before they are to be set out. The okra seedlings, after they have been weather-hardened by frequent exposure in the seed flat, can be set out on the frost-free date; the eggplant seedlings had better be set out a week or so later, when the sun has thoroughly warmed the soil. The okra plant will require two months to mature; the eggplant will mature in three or more months, reckoning from the time the seedling was set out.

Okra and eggplant do not require more than ordinary garden soil of adequate fertility and good drainage. The South is the natural home of these plants, where they are grown in the spring and fall. Farther north, they may be grown with luck, which means a long, warm growing season. In the extreme North, where the growing season is short, it is a rare triumph to bring either of these plants to maturity. Since both are bush-type plants that may reach a height of three feet, they require space. Set the plants about three feet apart.

SUMMER AND WINTER SQUASH. Of the several varieties of summer and winter squash, the one I strongly recommend to the gardener who has limited space is Italian vegetable marrow, commonly known as zucchini. (The correct Italian spelling is zucchine, "little pumpkins," the diminutive plural of the feminine noun *zucca,* "pumpkin.") I do this for several reasons. All squashes require too much space for what they yield. There is no particular reason for raising one's own hard-rind squash, such as the Hubbard, because it is a vegetable that, like the potato, is brought to full maturity for storage, and those grown in our own gardens would not be better than what we can buy. And squash is always inexpensive.

A better case can be made for the soft-rind summer squashes, since these, as so many other vegetables, are best when brought directly from the garden to the kitchen. The most desirable of them, since it can be prepared in a number of different and interesting ways, is zucchini. In all fairness, however, it ought to be noted that winter squash is richer in protein, minerals, and vitamins than the summer type.

All squashes are cultivated in substantially the same way. They may be grown in virtually all regions in ordinary garden soil that is fertile and well drained. They require plenty of moisture. In the very warm South, they can be grown in winter; but since they are sensitive to severe frost, their cultivation in other regions is limited to the growing season between late spring and early fall. No vegetable needs less attention than squash once the plant is started and well rooted.

A squash plant requires lots of space. Allow the zucchini plant a circular area five feet in diameter. Put five seeds at the center, an inch apart and arranged in a circle. When the plants are up, three or so inches long, and you can distinguish the weak from the strong, remove all but the two healthiest. As they grow, these will intertwine into a bushy group. Two such clumps will provide a continuous supply of zucchini all through the summer, more than a family can use. Cocozella (Italian marrow) is the best variety, though any other will be good enough. Proceed in the same way for the cultivation of any other type of squash.

Zucchini are actually cylindrical pumpkins, and if left to achieve seed maturity they will be as large as watermelons. They are at their best for the table when their color (light to deep green) is clean, their length from five to eight inches, and their skin can be easily pierced by very light pressure of one's thumbnail. There is another way of telling when they have passed their prime. Zucchini bear two kinds of large yellow blossoms: one is borne at the end of a long stem, as a flower; the other is attached to the end of the zucchini. When the latter begins to wilt, the zucchini is going over the hill. Take it, then, after it is several inches long and still in bloom.

SWEET CORN. How well do you like it? How fastidious are you about its quality? How large is your garden? These are questions to be asked, for sweet corn requires considerable space and the yield per unit of land is small. It is, however, one of those vegetables whose quality degenerates rapidly after harvest; so if you are addicted to it, enjoy the pleasure of eating corn within an hour after it is taken off the stalk. Corn is easy to grow in any type of tolerably good soil, in any region where the warm growing season lasts at least four months. Corn requires continuous warmth for germination and normal, vigorous growth. Burpee's Golden Bantam is the most highly recommended variety for the home garden.

Put down three seeds every twelve inches in a shallow

furrow and firm them down with an inch of screened soil. When the plants are a few inches long, thin them so that they are a foot apart. When they are a foot high, bank a little soil around them and keep them well watered. Remove all weeds as they appear. When the cobs are formed and filled with yellow kernels to the tip end, husk them and drop them in boiling water. Smear them with lots of butter, sprinkle with salt and pepper, and eat your fill.

A packet of seeds is enough for an eighty-foot row. A single stalk may produce two cobs, but no more. If you plant in short rows, space them three feet apart. In the South, sweet corn may be sown at three-week intervals from early spring until fall. Elsewhere, successive plantings are possible only where the growing season is four months or longer.

TOMATOES. Of all the warm-weather vegetables, the tomato is the most exacting in its sun requirements. After the plant is well established and begins to bloom, it will need at least two more months of sustained warmth. When such warm weather is only approximated, the plant will grow well enough, even luxuriantly, and bear fruit, but the tomato it yields will not be eaten with any relish by one who knows his tomatoes. A gallant ditchdigger friend of my early years, Leonard, who was as skilled at raising tomatoes as Mike was at raising peas, would not eat it at all. One glance at it and his face mirrored its vapid insipidity. That such a thing as that should be dignified by the name of tomato!

Leonard was a southern Italian, and like so many of his fellows, he could not live without tomatoes. And he knew tomatoes, even to the extent of knowing about them what was not known, so vivid was his imagination when the subject was *pomodoro*. "The tomato plant is a weed," he would

say, reflectively. "It grows better neglected, without cultivation. I saw one once growing on a rock pile, loaded with
perfect tomatoes. Who knows where the seed came from."
Was he reporting a fact? Was he dramatizing his wish to
be infallible as a grower of tomatoes? Fact or fancy,
Leonard knew tomatoes. He knew that a tomato such as he
could not live without had gloss, depth of color, resilient
solidity, and a dense juice that does not easily separate from
the pulp. "When you bite into a perfect tomato, there is no
drip," he used to say. "When the juice is thin and runny,
the tomato is watery. And the sweetness of a tomato, its
perfection of flavor, is of that special kind that results from
a nice balance of acid and vegetable sugar in the mature
fruit." He was right. And what I am trying to suggest is
that to produce such a tomato, constant sun is more important than soil fertility. Not burning heat, you understand,
but a robust, gentle, life-giving sun that keeps the thermome-
ter steady in the high 70's or low 80's.

In reciting these facts I am not trying to dissuade from
growing tomatoes those of you who live where summers are
cool; I am hoping, rather, to lessen your disappointment
should the sun fail to shine on your labor well done, as it
did on mine last season. I had luxuriant plants; there were
tomatoes on them; some turned a sickly red; none was such
as Leonard could not live without. Being his respectful
disciple, I left them to rot on the vine and managed to live
without them. But I am not easily discouraged; I shall try
my luck again next season.

Success in growing quality tomatoes thus depends largely
on the weather; soil type and condition are of secondary
importance. Lacking sun, a very fertile soil is likely to
produce a luxuriant plant and few tomatoes. In the lower
South, fine tomatoes can be grown even in the winter. In
other regions, where the growing season is three or four

months, tomato culture is limited to the summer months.

In growing tomatoes the common practice is to set out healthy, sturdy plants, about two months old, soon after the soil is warm and the danger of frost is past. One may produce his own plants, germinating the seeds in seed flats, but if he chooses to do this, he must sow the seed a good eight weeks before the date of the final frost—early in March where the plants are to be set out early in May. Is it worth the effort to proceed thus? I would say no. The home gardener is better advised to buy the plants he needs from the local nursery. A garden store or nursery will have healthy plants, produced by an expert, and such as are best adapted to the region.

The yield of the tomato plant per unit of land is considerable. A single vigorous plant may produce as many as ten pounds of tomatoes during the season. Therefore, the home gardener is not likely to require more than a dozen plants for the normal needs of his family; and if he needs less, the more reason for buying them rather than going to all the trouble of producing his own. And if he lacks space in his garden plot for even so few as a dozen, he can set out a plant here and there among his shrubs, against a house wall where there is plenty of sun, or even in one or two large pots on the patio or sun porch. All things considered, then, it is wise to buy the tomato plants one may need.

The tomato plant can be cultivated in one of two ways. As the plant develops toward maturity, and before the fruit begins to set, it proliferates into a main and several dependent vines. These may be left to bend and spread upon the ground. The result will be a low-lying, bushy plant of considerable spread. The alternative is to prune the lesser vines and support the main vine on a stout stake five feet long, driven well into the ground at the foot of the plant.

Tomato plants—staked and spread out

The first procedure is recommended for areas where sun is abundant and its heat intense. The tomatoes, resting on the ground or hanging near it on the vines, will be protected from the scorching sun. Pruning to a single vine and staking is the procedure recommended for cooler regions, where the plant requires the full benefit of what sun there may be. When the main vine is supported on a stake, tiny shoots at the axil of leaf and stem will appear on it from time to time. These are parasitical growths and should be pinched off as soon as they appear.

There are many varieties of tomatoes, including the yellow kind, the pear-shaped, and the cherry. It would be idle to name them all, since a given variety is usually adapted to a given area. The gardener is well advised to plant the variety recommended by his seed merchant or nurseryman.

And now, a final word. When your first tomato is ripe, and conforms to the description of a tomato such as Leonard could not live without, take salt and pepper and go to the garden. Pluck the fruit of your labor from the vine. The sun will be hot and the tomato warm. Cut it in quarters, sprinkle it with salt and pepper, and pop it, a quarter at a time, into your mouth. I shall be listening for your sighs of sweet contentment!

CELERY. Crisp November and crisp celery! Was there ever a generalization more definitive? In May we gather nuts, in June we mow the field, cutting the cool green grass when prime for discriminating ruminants, and in November we cut our celery for the table.

I have known celery for as long as I can remember, but I had not heard of Utah celery until I married a young lady whose home was in Salt Lake City. On the Thanksgiving following our marriage, and for every Thanksgiving thereafter, my wife's father sent us a gift package of Utah celery, four huge, nicely blanched bunches wrapped in moist paper tightly tucked in a cardboard container and brought to our door by the trucker from Railway Express. The gift vivified a fact of which I must have been vaguely aware: that the fall was the season for the finest celery. And I learned also that, whereas Idaho has its potato, Utah is proud of its celery. And justly so, for the stalks of Utah celery are thicker, more round than flat, more thoroughly blanched, more crackling to the bite, and less stringy than other varieties. There must be something in the soil of Utah that makes it particularly congenial to the cultivation of that variety known commercially as Utah 52-70.

Celery is a cool-weather vegetable; therefore, it can be grown in the early spring or in the late fall. In the lower South it can be grown in the winter. In the colder regions of the North it can be grown in the summer. The consequence is that it is always available in the vegetable bins of the supermarket. But he who is aware of such trivial matters may remember that he has always had the finest celery in the fall. It is for this reason that I did not include it in the group of cold-hardy plants cultivated in the early spring for late spring and early summer harvest. Wanting only the best, I have chosen to include it in the group of vegetables seeded when the spring season is well advanced and harvested in the fall and early winter.

Celery can be grown by the home gardener, but not as easily as beans and cabbage and squash. Germination of celery seed is so slow that the inexperienced gardener may fret with impatience when he sees no sign of sprouting weeks after he has sown the seed. It may take as long as ten or more weeks, the time required for radishes to mature, to start celery plants from seed. Little celery seedlings are very fragile; they must be cultivated with care. The total time required from seedling to plant maturity may be as long as five months, notwithstanding that the seed packet may have indicated four months or less. The soil in which the celery plant is to mature must be fine, rich, loose, loamy, and meticulously prepared. When the plant is well on its way to maturity, its tender, succulent center may attract a host of gluttonous aphids; these must be sprayed out of existence with an appropriate insecticide suggested by the local seed dealer. Thus, as for all other good things, one must pay for his celery with diligence and care.

All things considered, the gardener who wants to raise a couple dozen bunches of celery may want to buy the little plants at a nursery. Or, with a packet of seeds, you can start enough plants for an acre of celery. Prepare a three-foot-square seed bed of finely screened soil; scatter the seeds on it as evenly as possible, barely cover them with a thin layer of sand well mixed with peat moss, and sprinkle the bed with water, keeping it moist thereafter as necessary. When the seedlings are an inch long, thin them so that each one may have about an inch of space. When the plants are well formed and four to six inches long, they are ready to be transplanted to the area where the celery plant is to mature.

And here one must proceed with care. I have already indicated that the soil must be rich and of fine texture to a considerable depth. A week or so before the celery plants are to be set out, prepare a furrow about eight inches deep. For a fifty-foot row of celery, about sixty plants, mix two wheelbarrows of rotted manure and three pounds of a balanced garden fertilizer. Spread the mixture evenly along the bottom of the furrow and cover it with two or three inches of fine soil. Don't hurry. Work with care. Leave nothing undone that should be done, and you will raise gold-medal celery! On a cool day, or late in the afternoon, pinch off the tip ends of the outer leaves of the largest celery plants in the seed bed. Soak the bed thoroughly; take up each plant carefully so that the roots are not torn, place it in a hole in the furrow, and firm the soil on its roots with the hands. Space the plants ten inches apart. Water them regularly so that they may have plenty of moisture.

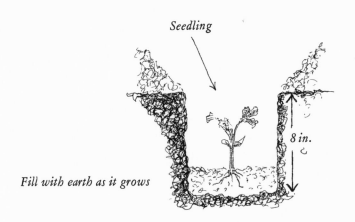

Seedling

Fill with earth as it grows

8 in.

When the plants are rooted in it, the eight-inch-deep furrow will be better than half filled. When the plants have attained a height of about ten inches, draw a bit more soil into the furrow, about an inch, and bank it carefully around each plant, being careful not to push it onto its tender center. Repeat the procedure at intervals as the plants develop toward maturity until the furrow is filled. The purpose of banking is twofold: it provides the large root system of the celery plant the moist soil covering it requires, and it blanches the bottom of the celery stalks by excluding them from light. When the plants are nearing maturity, fifteen to eighteen inches tall, the stalks may be further blanched by wrapping the lower two thirds with newspaper secured with heavy twine.

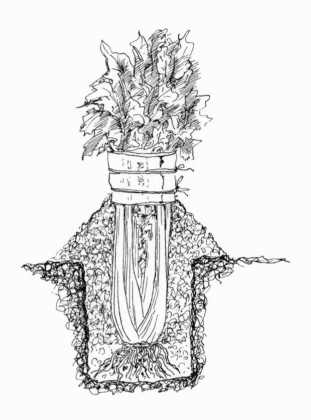

That is all there is to growing celery. Seed sown in mid-May, the seedlings transplanted in mid-July, will produce celery for your Thanksgiving dinner. And as you crunch it in gratitude you may remember that my discovery of the finest celery grown in America was the consequence of my successful courtship of a Utah belle. Had I gone a-wooing in Denver rather than in Salt Lake City, I might have had to live out my days with only ordinary celery to go with my bread and cheese.

Group Two.
Plant the Following Vegetables Two Weeks After
Frost-Free Date.

PEPPERS. We live in a region where a cool and moist spring passes imperceptibly into a summer that is normally cool, the temperature seldom, and then only for brief periods, rising to the middle 8o's: a region ideal for the cultivation of most leaf and root vegetables but generally unsuited to the raising of those that require months of sustained heat. So when we indulge our passion for growing such hot-weather plants as peppers, we do so as gamblers steeled against failure. Peppers do not compromise: it's either heat or no dice. Two seasons ago, when our summer was the hottest on record, the pepper plants blossomed as they do in hot Calabria; last season, the coolest on record, it was no dice. But we, whose addiction to peppers is total, are un-daunted; we shall try again next season.

The southern latitudes are the congenial habitat of the pepper family. There they can be grown throughout the spring and summer, and even in the fall in some of the hotter areas. Elsewhere it is utterly futile to set out pepper plants until the ground is warm; and once they are rooted, neither meticulous cultivation nor the tenderest loving care will coax them to maturity without months of clear skies and hot sun.

Given heat, their demands on the gardener will be no more exacting than those of ordinary cabbage. The seed of the pepper is very much like that of the tomato; and he who wants to start his own plants may proceed according to the directions given for tomatoes. The soil need not be too rich; any type that is adequate for other vegetables will do for peppers. The plant is low and bushy but not too large.

Give it a circular area fifteen inches in diameter, keep it watered, and pray for sun.

As blubber is the special food of the Eskimo, so are peppers, in all their varieties, an indispensable element in the diet of hot-country people such as the Spanish, the Mexican, the southern Italian. They eat many kinds of peppers and in great quantities, but they especially relish the hot varieties. These hot-blooded, fiery-tempered people! Do they require the fire of peppers and other hot food to match the fire in their blood? Do they actually enjoy eating peppers so hot that they would blister the lips of any mortal outside the pepper-eating clan? Or is the eating thereof an act of self-immolation, a hangover from the days of the medieval flagellants? Or a rite, perhaps, in self-proof, a trial by fire?

I have often wondered. For one thing is certain: the peppers they eat with apparent relish are so hot that no outsider can endure them. I have heard more than one southern Italian insist that the peppers he was eating were not hot, yet as he denied their fire there were beads of perspiration on his forehead and his eyes were moist with disciplined tears. "No, no! They are not really hot! Or, perhaps, one might say they are just a little bit hot. . . ." Well, it was that special sort of little that goes a long way.

And yet there is much to say in behalf of peppers, especially the hot varieties, as food; they are delicious and marvelously nutritious. This may astonish you, but it is a fact: one ounce of a dry hot pepper contains more minerals and vitamins than four ounces of an ordinary green bell pepper. Having recorded this fact I shall make no more of it and simply urge one to grow peppers for fun and eat them for pleasure.

There are many varieties of peppers, and they do not all taste alike. The two main classes are the hot and the mild, and there are several varieties in each class. The Tabasco and the Long Red Cayenne are the best known and the most fiery of the hot group; the California Wonder and the Yale Wonder are common varieties of the mild bell pepper. But there are many more in each class, and some that are only mildly hot. There are red, green, and yellow peppers. Some are short and conical, or squat and round, the size of an apricot. There are long, pointed pods, varying in diameter at the stem end from three quarters of an inch to an inch and a half. And have you ever seen the tiny green peppers, no larger than your little finger, preserved in vinegar? The Italians call them *peperoncini*. And have you ever had them fresh, sautéed in olive oil with a touch of garlic?

No, you probably haven't. And the reason is that Americans, except in certain parts of the South and in some localities in the East, have a limited acquaintance with peppers. The fact is regrettable, but I don't know what can be done. Seed stores offer only the varieties I have named; and without seed . . . Well, without seed, the gardener who would explore the total good that is in peppers will have to find them somewhere, somehow. Let him inquire, as I did, at the homes of Spaniards, Mexicans, and southern Italians until he finds one among them who is a gardener and has the seed. I found three such, and now I can eat fairly hot peppers without beading my brow.

CUCUMBERS. In passing from the hot pepper to the cool cucumber we are still in the land of the sun, for the cucumber is definitely a warm-weather vegetable. After the last frost and when the sun has warmed the ground, the cucumber seed may be safely sown. If the temperature does not fall below 70°F., germination will be fairly rapid. Thereafter, the plant will require warmth though not heat. The plant is as sensitive to extreme heat as it is to even a mild frost. Therefore, where summers are excessively hot, cucumbers can be grown only in the spring; in other regions, where they are grown throughout the summer, they will succumb to the first frost of fall.

A cucumber vine requires considerable space, but its yield is abundant. Two or three hills, with two vines to each hill, will yield enough cucumbers for a family. The cultivation of the cucumber is the same as that for summer squash.

BLACK-EYED PEAS. These are also known as southern table peas and cowpeas. They are very nutritious and very tasty, so it is a pity that they are well known and appreciated only in the South and among people of Mediterranean origin. Black-eyed peas require as much heat as peppers. Hence, their cultivation is pretty much limited to the South and other regions where summers are hot and the growing season long. Along the Northwest coast they will come to maturity only when the spring and summer are exceptionally warm.

I have no idea why they are called peas, for they are more akin to beans. The pod is roundish, somewhat like that of a young Blue Lake green bean, about eight inches long and pointed. Its color is a dense green. Italians call them "little beans with eyes." Which is precisely what they are, shaped like a kidney. They are excellent eaten as green beans, more grassy than any of the green-bean varieties. They are also eaten fresh-shelled out of the pod as one eats peas. But most people who eat black-eyed peas use the dry sort. This multipurpose plant that produces food so tasty and nutritious should be grown by every gardener who lives in hot country and has the space. The plant is a low-growing bush cultivated in the same way as bush beans. Why not give it a go?

ह

And now a pause in our labor so that we may have a look at what we have done and plan for what remains to be done. Assuming that you have been with me all the way, and that the group of vegetables we have considered in this chapter are bedded and growing, where are we? What have we ventured? We have seeded more than a score of herbaceous edibles; and, as the seasons flow, we are in the first month of summer. There is yet space in our garden, and I have more recommendations to make. Some of the early crops, such as radishes, peas, lettuce, spinach, may be already, or soon to be, harvested, and the land thus released will be available for further cultivation. Continuous production is our aim right down to the last day of the growing season.

Therefore, plan accordingly. Rake the soil, or spade it if necessary, and remove all weeds. Scatter some fertilizer on it and work it in with the rake. Stake out your unused domain and plan where you will sow the group of vegetables that I shall suggest for your cultivation and pleasure in the next chapter.

NINE

Rounding Out the Harvest

The poet will forgive us if we say that a kitchen garden is a joy forever! It is surely a convenience. He who grows his own need not rush off to the grocery for the sprig of parsley he needs at the very last moment to enhance his omelet. Nor is there any doubt that it is a means of saving on the grocery bill. A small plot of land, judiciously cultivated, will yield a greater return in dollars and cents than would appear to one who does not know how immensely productive a bit of land can be. Gardening is also fruitful exercise and recreation for men and women who enjoy working with their hands on the land; and it provides the produce one likes, always fresh and always prime for the table.

These are the pleasures and advantages afforded by a kitchen garden, and there is no need to urge them further. I restate them here only that I may hold in relief against them two others as noteworthy, though not so pat: the little patch of land that one so wisely reserved for growing one's peas and carrots becomes, imperceptibly, a little horticultural laboratory, and a means of enlarging both one's range and one's appreciation of herbaceous edibles. When these ends have been achieved, one has rounded out the harvest and may properly regard himself as the complete kitchen gardener.

When one first decides to build a garden, he will likely have in mind growing the more common vegetables that are normally consumed in his region and that are indigenous to it. And that is precisely what he will do. Working with care, and as he adds to his experience, he will observe, perhaps for the first time in his life, the miracle of seed into fruit. Amazed by his success with cabbage—was there ever one so lovely and so perfect?—and perhaps taking unto himself even that credit which was properly nature's due, he will begin to wonder whether his thumb isn't actually greener than green. And properly so! Remembering that he was counseled not to abide too strictly by the weather data of his region, he will venture to grow an eggplant where one has never grown before. Luck with him all the way, he will succeed. And the amateur who began by growing peas and carrots, refining his ingenuity and giving full scope to his imagination, will be well on his way to becoming the complete gardener.

Well on his way; but not quite arrived. Before he may wear the crown of leeks, he must give proof that he is as accomplished at the table as he is in the garden. Using the garden as a horticultural laboratory, he has gone beyond growing peas and carrots and enlarged his vegetable spectrum; he must now give proof that he has enlarged his taste and eats with relish of all that he grows.

I therefore offer myself as your guide once more and ask you to consider experimenting with another group of vegetables, an even gardener's dozen. Some of these you may not know at all; most of them you will know in a casual sort of way. But a casual acquaintance is not enough; I ask you to know them intimately, in the garden and at the table, as you surely will once you have made them your dearly begotten. At the head of the list is the cardoon. Have you ever seen one? Let me tell about it.

CARDOONS. In the botanical literature the cardoon is known as *Cynara cardunculus,* a member of the large family of *Compositae.* The name derives from the Latin *carduus,* "thistle." And that is precisely what the cardoon is, a domesticated thistle. Once planted and left to its own devices, it will grow year after year exactly as a thistle. As the plant develops from a seed very much like that of the sunflower, the young shoot forms a cluster of rosette leaves, and from the center of these the stem rises. At maturity it may attain a height of six feet. At its end, and at the end of its several lateral branches, a purple-centered flower bud develops, very like that of a thistle but of great size and striking beauty. That is the seed pod, crammed with hundreds of seeds. Its life cycle completed, the stem withers and dies. The following spring new shoots emerge from the woody root crown. Thus, the cardoon is an herbaceous perennial, and its edible portion is the lower part of the leafy stalk. The stalks are huge and fern-like in structure, the large outer ones in the rosette often attaining a length of five feet. The lower third is bare and fleshy like the stalk of a celery. The upper portion flares out in leafy serrated notches on both sides of the central spine. When the plant is full grown, it looks like a huge tropical fern, the outer stalks arched gracefully away from the center on all sides, and the inner ones clustered closely and growing straight and pointed. When all the stalks are bound together in a bundle, the cardoon resembles a celery such as Gulliver may have seen in the land of the Brobdingnagians. And, like celery, it's the inner stalks that one eats. As one peels off and works toward the center, one finds the inner core, crisp, solid, bleached, bittersweet, and succulent. Left alone after the plant has reached maturity for the table, it sends forth the flowering stem from that inner core.

I have no idea how the cardoon came into being. It is native to the Mediterranean, where it has been prized as a vegetable for centuries. In the thistle family there are two kinds well known in most regions of America. One has leaves formed pretty much like those of the cardoon, though much smaller; the other has leaves somewhat like those of the rhubarb plant. The latter kind is sometimes called the wild cardoon. Its stalks are edible and very good when they are young and tender, early in the spring. It may well be that long ago, in some garden of Eden, the cardoon was born of the happy commingling of these two thistles. Whatever its parentage, the issue is most certainly distinguished.

Propagation of the cardoon is by seed, and though the plant itself is cold-hardy, germination requires warmth. The proper time for sowing will depend on where one lives. Where, as in the South and along the Pacific coast, the growing season extends into the fall or early winter, the cardoon can be sown late in May or early in June. In those regions the plant will attain table maturity at about Thanksgiving. In latitudes where the growing season is shorter, such as New England, the seed can be sown early in the spring, as soon as the ground is warm. The mature plant will be ready for the table early in the fall. Thus, at some time or other, the cardoon can be grown in every region in America.

This exquisite vegetable is cultivated in the same way as celery, since it, too, must be blanched to make it more tender. The furrow into which the seeds are bedded, two every 3 feet, should be at least 10 inches deep. Cover the seeds with an inch of screened soil. After germination and when the little plants are 3 to 4 inches long, do whatever thinning is necessary to provide 3 feet of space between plants. When

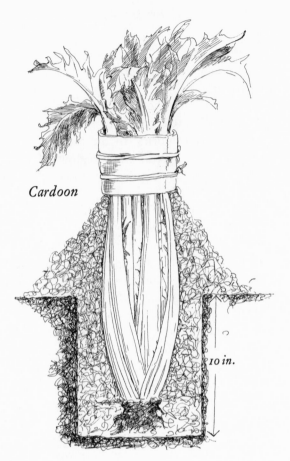

Cardoon

10 in.

*To protect cardoon from freezing weather,
wrap with newspaper and cover with soil*

they are a foot long, begin banking them by drawing soil into the furrow (see page 187). Continue banking at intervals of about three weeks, depending upon the rate of growth, until the plant is full grown. It may then be 2 feet in circumference near the base and 3 or 4 feet long. At that stage the lower portion should be well banked, as it will be if the soil was periodically heaped into the furrow as directed. Thus banked, the lower portion of the stalks will be blanched. To blanch them further above the ground, the plant must be wrapped two thirds of the way to the top. For this purpose, use newspapers, burlap, or some heavy plastic material, bundling the plant snugly and securing the wrapping with heavy twine. In two or three weeks the entire cardoon will be blanched and ready for the table.

Although the plant is cold-hardy, it will not survive a deadly freeze. Temperatures in the low 30's or high 20's will not harm the plant. Where I live we had a cold spell in late December. There was snow and the temperature dropped to a few degrees below freezing, but the cardoons survived unprotected. Where there is the possibility that the freeze may be more deadly, the cardoon can be protected in one of two ways. You can add to the wrapping that was done for blanching; thus bundled, the plant will survive temperatures in the low twenties. To protect it against a deeper freeze, wrap and bundle the plant as described above; then, beginning at the root, dig a trench about a foot deep and as long as two thirds of the plant's length. This done, loosen the soil all around the root, and bend the plant down, and lay it in the trench. Here you must proceed with care so that the long taproot is not broken. Since the plant is longer than the trench, the leaf ends will extend beyond it. Tuck more newspapers or other wrapping around the bundled plant and cover it with a foot or so of soil, leaving the leafy ends exposed so that the plant may continue to breathe. This burial will protect the plant against very harsh weather, and so long as the ground remains fairly dry, the cardoon will remain in excellent condition for several weeks, ready for use as one needs it.

A cardoon tastes somewhat like an artichoke, but sweeter. The inner core, like the heart of celery, is crisp and solid; it is often eaten raw. It is in no way a vegetable for which one must cultivate a taste. Having tasted the cardoon once, anyone who likes good food and is not suspicious of that which is new to him is likely to enjoy it immediately. Such has been the experience at our table. Everyone has liked the cardoon very much on first trial. So why not give it a go and see what success you can have with it in your region?

ARTICHOKES. This vegetable, definitely gourmet food, always expensive, was developed from the cardoon. The two look so much alike as bush-like plants that only a trained eye can tell them apart. We know that the artichoke was well known and highly prized as a vegetable several centuries before Christ; so if it was developed from the cardoon, the latter must have a history as long as that of the grape.

Native to southern Europe, the artichoke was cultivated around Naples in the fifteenth century, whence its culture gradually extended to other regions along the Mediterranean. It was introduced into the United States at the beginning of the nineteenth century, and by 1899 French and Italian immigrants were cultivating it commercially in Louisiana and California. At the present time, the entire crop of globe artichokes in the United States comes from six coastal counties in California.

Like the parent cardoon, the globe artichoke, *Cynara scolymus,* is a herbaceous perennial of the thistle family. The plant attains a height of 3 to 4 feet and a leaf spread

Perfect artichoke

Artichoke, past its prime

of 5 to 6 feet. A single root crown three or four years old will send up as many as a dozen substantial shoots. Each one forms a basal cluster or rosette leaves, formed like those of the cardoon, though smaller and less fleshy at the base. A stem with several branches rises gradually from the center of the rosette cluster. While the plant is growing toward maturity, a flower bud is formed at the tip of the main stem and, later, at the tip end of the several branches. These, in their mature state, before flowers and seeds develop, are the edible portions of the plant. These are the artichokes.

Thus the artichoke, like asparagus, beans, and broccoli, is actually the seed pod of the plant. And it has an interesting structure. The bud, when prime for the table, is a compact mass of bracts, or scales, closely overlaid one upon another and attached at their base to a round, fleshy receptacle upon which flower and seeds are borne at maturity. The receptacle is slightly concave. The bracts are roughly pear-shaped. They are small on the underside of the receptacle where it is attached to the stem, become larger as they grow upward all around it, and decrease in size as they reach the receptacle's rim. When the artichoke is at its best for the table, the bracts are closed tightly into a compact, ovoid bud about the size of a large lemon. As it develops toward maturity, the bracts open at the top like the petals of a rosebud, and the artichoke becomes a purple-centered, thistle-like flower with a seed receptacle four to six inches in diameter. At that stage its appeal is purely aesthetic, and the gardener gladly yields it to the flower-garden buff who will use it in his flower arrangements.

It is necessary to understand the structure and development of the artichoke in order to use it wisely in the kitchen, for it, like asparagus and broccoli, belongs to that class of herbaceous plants that are edible only when they are immature. A full-grown cabbage is still edible, and so is the dried bean in the pod; but an artichoke that is full grown, or nearly so, is not good for the table. Hence the importance of knowing when to harvest it.

The artichoke is generally at its best when it is about two thirds its normal size at maturity; it is at this stage of development that it is brought to market in artichoke country, often with a long stem, so it looks like a big green rosebud. However, regardless of size, an artichoke is in excellent condition so long as its bracts are tightly closed at the apex. When these begin to open, the artichoke has passed its prime. Beware, then, of large artichokes with loose bracts open at the top. Much of it will be inedible; it will be tough and bitterish; at its center there will be a considerable "choke," the cottony fluff that is the mass of flowers well on the way to development and that emerges only when the bud has passed its prime.

The reader who is artichoke-wise will forgive me for going into such detail in describing the structure of the artichoke, but unless it is cut at the proper time and properly handled, it is of no consequence at all. An overgrown globe artichoke, mercilessly boiled so that much of its goodness is sent to the sewer, its bracts then dipped in butter and nibbled uncertainly at the ends, may well leave the meat-and-potatoes man wondering. And that is precisely the way the artichoke is too often prepared for the table. It was probably such an overaged and overcooked artichoke that provoked a judgment attributed to Lord Chesterfield: "The artichoke is the only vegetable known of which there is more left when one has finished eating it than when he began." I quote from memory; but that is the substance of what he said. And it reveals that the good lord himself had not been properly introduced to that Mediterranean delicacy.

Taken in its prime, the artichoke may be trimmed, cut in halves or quarters, cooked as one likes it, and eaten as any other vegetable. There will be nothing left on the plate to feed the wit of a Lord Chesterfield.

So much for its history and structure. Now a word about the cultivation of the artichoke. Contrary to what many people believe, it is not a hot-country plant. It thrives in a mild, sunny climate, requires a soil that is loose and rich to a considerable depth, for its roots are long and branched. In such an environment, and where winters are free of deadly freeze, the plant will produce edible buds in the spring and the fall. West of the Rocky Mountains and in the South, it will yield a crop in the spring. In regions where winters are very severe, the plant can be saved for spring resurgence by heaping ten or so inches of soil over the root crown. This "mulching" is a means generally employed to save the roots of plants in regions where the ground freezes to a considerable depth in the winter.

Propagation of the artichoke is either by seed, rooted shoots, or by transplanting sections of rootstalks taken from an established plant. Since rootstalks and rooted shoots may not be readily available, the home gardener who is anxious to try his luck at growing artichokes will have to use seeds. Trace a shallow furrow, drop three or four seeds in it at intervals of at least three feet, and cover them with an inch of screened soil. This should be done early in the spring when the ground is warm. When the seeds have sprouted and the plants are four or five inches long, remove all but one from each group. Water them regularly. When the plants are about eighteen inches long, work into the soil around each plant a shovelful of barnyard manure or a cup of commercial fertilizer. Do not expect a crop the first season. Before the plant will bear edible buds, its ample root crown must be well developed.

As already noted, the artichoke plant is a perennial. It will send up new shoots each spring from an enduring root crown. When these appear the second season, and every spring thereafter, remove all but the three sturdiest. As the season progresses the plants will develop a central stem, which will bear from six to a dozen buds. When it is through bearing and the artichoke is harvested, the stem is cut at ground level and one awaits the next season's shoots and the next crop. That is all there is to the cultivation of artichokes. Remember, however, that during the budding season the plant must be kept well watered. If there is a moisture deficiency the buds will be dwarfish and loose rather than plump and compact.

Commercial growers renew the plant every four or five years. The root crown is dug up and a section of it is re-planted. The reason for this is that old plants tend to revert to their thistle ancestry. I do not know why; but that it is so I have noted in my own garden. Plants that I have left to age have not done so well as those I have renewed. I have been growing artichokes for two decades. Having done all that I advise you to do, we have had our fill of prime artichokes every season. There is no reason why you, with equal diligence, cannot do what I have done. Will you give it a go and prove that my faith in you is well rooted?

GARDEN ROCKET. This is a delightful salad green used in blending green salads in much the same way as cress and sorrel are used. Its botanical name is *Eruca sativa,* and it is one of the various members of the *Cruciferae,* the mustard family. The plant somewhat resembles young spinach; its flavor is pungent, pleasantly sourish, and mus-tardy. Those who like it very much, as I do, do not hesitate to use it as the principal ingredient in a green salad. Others prefer to use it more sparingly, to the same effect that they use other spicy additions to a green salad, such as parsley, chives, and cress.

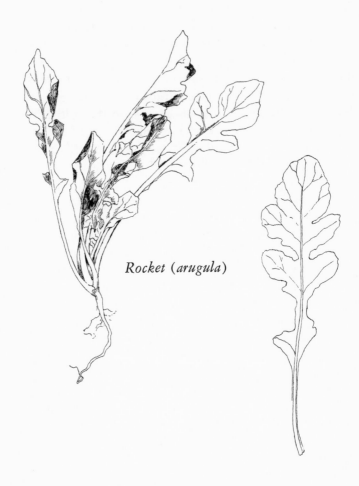

Rocket (arugula)

In whatever amounts used, it lifts a green salad above the ordinary and it ought to be more widely known than it is. I learned about garden rocket at a luncheon several years ago at the home of Rosa Mondavi, who is president of the Charles Krug Winery in Napa Valley, California. An excellent cook in the best Italian tradition, she asked me whether

I knew what it was that she was eating heartily while
cutting greens into the salad bowl. She gave me a taste, and
I ate it no less heartily than she; and when I left, her brother,
Zio Nenno, a very complete gardener who wears a crown
of both leeks and garlic, gave me a handful of garden-
rocket seeds. I have had it growing profusely in my garden
ever since.

Of all herbaceous plants, it is the easiest to cultivate and
the least exacting in its soil requirements. Scatter the seeds
on a patch of ground, work them into the soil with the
prongs of a rake; a little water and a little sun will do the
rest. Germination is rapid; the life cycle of the plant is brief.
In two and a half months it will go to seed. To have a
continuous supply throughout the growing season, one
ought to do successive sowings of it at intervals of four
weeks. The seeds from the first crop can be used for the
later sowings.

Garden-rocket seed may not be easy to find. If your seed
dealer does not have it on hand, he may be able to procure
it elsewhere. If he fails, and you are intent on attaining your
crown, continue the search. There are herbalists around the
country; write to the Horticultural Division of your state
college.

ॐ

I come now to a group of vegetables that are both cold-
hardy and tolerant of heat. Accordingly, these may be
planted either very early in the spring for summer harvest,
or in midsummer for harvest in the fall and early winter.
Those of us who live in regions where gardening is possible
only in the spring and summer will do our planting of these
as early in the spring as we can get on the land; those who
live in latitudes where the growing season extends into the
fall and early winter can plant them both in early spring

and midsummer. However, most of these vegetables are improved by exposure to the crisp weather of fall and early winter, so it is recommended that they be grown in the later season where it is possible to do so. The advice is especially relevant to the gardener who has a choice of seasons but who, for lack of space, can grow these vegetables only once. I have chosen to deal with them in this chapter because they are of the group of vegetables that many readers may know only casually or not at all—and that ought to be better known and better appreciated.

SAVOY CABBAGE. Have you ever seen one? The Savoy cabbage is as little known as the artichoke. One may have seen it and passed it by at the produce market for the reason that it did not look familiar, though it seemed to be a cabbage. And so it is. However, it differs from the familiar head of cabbage in several ways. Ordinary cabbage is white or a very pale green; Savoy cabbage is a deep, dense green. The Savoy's leaves are wrinkled, whereas the leaves of the other are smooth. A head of cabbage is solid; there is no give to the press of the fingertips. The head of a Savoy is more loose; it is resilient to the touch. A head of cabbage comes to market bald, completely trimmed; the Savoy head usually comes with its surrounding ruff of green leaves and these, when the head is garden-fresh, as it shall be for you henceforth and forevermore, are arched gracefully inward. Thus, when the two heads are placed side by side and submitted to the visual and tactile test, the Savoy appears to be a cabbage-no-cabbage. And what does the taste test reveal? The outer leaves of the savoy are decidedly herbaceous, grassy in flavor; the inner leaves, folded into a head, are more tender, sweeter, and milder than ordinary cabbage.

The plant is named after a region in southeastern France, near the Italian-Swiss border, called Savoy. Perhaps the variety originated there, a plausible supposition, since Savoy cabbage is highly esteemed in Lombardy, an Italian region not far from the Swiss border. In Italy, however, Savoy cabbage is called *cavolo verzotto,* "green cabbage."

The method of cultivation is like that of cabbage. What I said of most of the vegetables in this group, that they improve by exposure to fall and early winter weather, is especially true of Savoy cabbage. Like celery, it is of the season of mists and mellow fruitfulness. There is something in the declining sun, in the gradual cooling of the earth

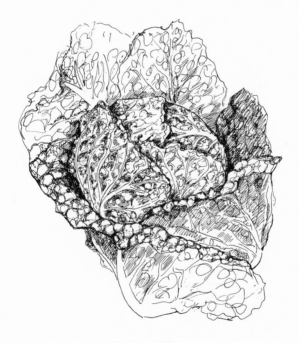

Savoy cabbage

after the heat of summer, that promotes in certain herbaceous edibles the very best that is latent in them. The proof of this is in the eating of the heart, neat and raw, of a savoy cabbage taken from the garden with its green leaves sparkling with a late November frost!

So, if you live in a region where the growing season extends into the fall and early winter, sow Savoy cabbage seed in a yard square of ground late in May. Remember to treat the soil with Diazinon or some other dust effective against the cabbage maggot. Germination will be prompt. Near the end of June, when the plants are five or six inches long, transplant them, giving each a circular area two feet in diameter, and cultivate them as you did the early spring cabbage. Once rooted and kept well watered, the Savoy plants will grow merrily in the summer sun. Be on the alert for aphis, the sucking villains who have a taste for Savoy cabbage, and destroy them with an appropriate spray as soon as they appear. Nature will tend to the rest. In November the Savoy cabbage will be ready for the table.

Begin the harvest soon after the cool autumn weather sets in, while the Savoy is still leafy and the head but partially formed, so that you can enjoy the fruit of your labor for as long a season as possible. As the weather becomes progressively cooler and the head develops further, the Savoy will not degenerate. By the mysterious chemistry of its being, perfectly at home in the cooler weather, it will consolidate its virtues and maintain them until the first merciless freeze of winter, which even Savoy cabbage cannot survive.

And even then, all may not be lost. Late one December, here where I live, winter came upon us with unexpected fury. The temperature dropped to 10° F. The broccoli, the sprouts, the Savoy cabbages, and all else in the garden were frozen to the core. Undaunted, I bundled myself in Eskimo togs and went to the garden with basket and cutting tool.

If man can freeze vegetables and thus preserve them for the table, why not nature? The cutting tool was unnecessary. With my bare hands I snapped off the broccoli tips as easily as if they were icicles; and as easily the Brussels sprouts were snapped off the stem. With a nudge of my boot the Savoy cabbage cracked free of the earth. I brought the frozen harvest to the kitchen. With considerable anxiety—after all, a great deal was at stake—I cleaned the broccoli first and dropped them immediately into salted water that I had put on to boil. They were the secondary buds, the ones that grow at the axil of the leaf and stem, quite small and tender; so they cooked very quickly. I lifted one with a fork and ate it hot from the pot with no further condiment than the salt that was in the water. Approaching it with fear that the broccoli might be a total loss, I was amazed at how good it was! So we had broccoli for dinner. I gave the sprouts and Savoy cabbage the same treatment. Since my wife is very fond of Brussels sprouts, I let her taste the first one. Very good! We rejoiced together and served them to our guests on New Year's Eve as an accompaniment to a great Shamrock ham. Nothing was lost! The Savoy cabbage I cooked and froze once more in its own juice. It will be used later in making minestrone.

Was nothing at all lost to winter's savage attack? Were these excellent vegetables as good after nature's freeze as they had been before? Well, my good friend, ask not such unkind questions; permit a begetter some degree of enthusiasm for his dearly begotten! In any case, it was a salvage operation undertaken on an inspired hunch, and it paid off mightily.

CHICORY. He who has never heard of cardoons, and whose acquaintance with Savoy cabbage is only casual, very likely does not know chicory as a vegetable at all. Hence my determination to bring the two together in the hope that the meeting will ripen into an enduring and happy union, for this indubitably illustrious member of the *Compositae*, the largest family of seed-bearing plants, many of which are common weeds, is much esteemed by the French and Italians, people who are at the top of the gastronomic scale. My own fondness for chicory approaches addiction.

The professional herbalist would place chicory, *Cichorium intybus*, in the class of wild potherbs. And chicory is, in fact, wild and a weed. The Italians call it *cicoria selvatica* and *radicchio;* the French name is *chicorée sauvage.* In America, where it was introduced from Europe as a weed, it is variously called succory, coffeeweed, blue sailors, and bunk. It is a perennial with a very long taproot, a rosette of serrated leaves about eight inches long, and a branched flowering stem that often reaches a height of six feet. The flowers borne along the stem, singly or in clusters of two or three on short stems, are round, about an inch in diameter, and the brightest, loveliest blue one has ever seen in nature's garden. The reader may have seen chicory in bloom in the northeastern states, where it grows in profusion, and elsewhere in hay fields and along the shoulders of country roads.

The horticulturist and botanist have perfected several domestic varieties of chicory, and it is with some of these that we are concerned. One is the large-rooted chicory, developed principally for its edible roots. Another is called witloof, white leaf; it was developed both for the edible root and leaves. A third variety is called Italian dandelion or asparagus chicory. The Italians call it *catalogna,* and thus relate it to Catalonia, a region in northeastern Spain. Treviso, near Venice, is very likely the chicory center of the world. The varieties developed there could be the subject for a considerable monograph. However, since the three varieties

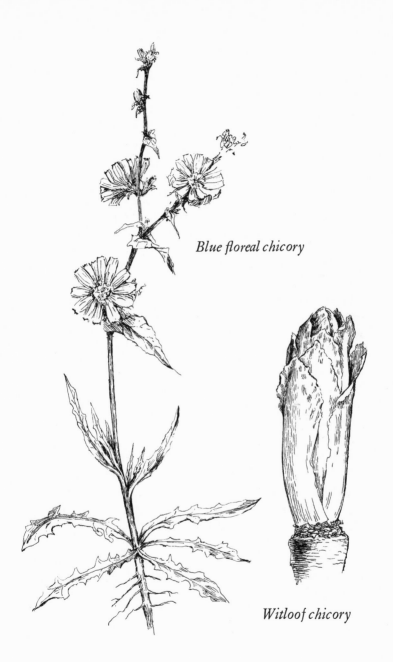

Blue floreal chicory

Witloof chicory

here named are the only ones the home gardener in America may find at his seed store, we shall deal only with them. If you live near Boston, New York, Philadelphia, or in any other large city where there are still well-defined ethnic centers, inquire about chicory in seed stores catering to people of Italian, French, or Spanish origin.

Chicory is cultivated primarily as a salad green. The root, much like that of the parsnip, is also eaten as a vegetable, both raw and cooked. Roasted and ground into a fine powder, it is used to flavor coffee—or to adulterate it. The proportions used vary from one to five ounces of chicory for every pound of coffee. Both the leaves and the root of the chicory, whether eaten raw or cooked, are good only when they are young. For the leaves, this means when they are about a third or half their normal length, which is twelve inches or slightly more. The roots are at their best when the plant is about full-grown in the spring; they are still good, however, until the time the plant begins to develop its flowering stem. Thereafter, like the carrot, the turnip, and certain other root vegetables, the root becomes progressively tough, woody, bitter, and generally unfit for the table.

He who eats chicory for the first time must be prepared for a mildly bitter taste—pleasant for all who have a bitter rather than a sweet tooth—and distinct flavor. Perhaps one may have to learn to like it; if so he must persevere, remembering that it comes highly recommended by people noted for the excellence of their cuisine.

The three varieties named are at once cold-hardy and tolerant of heat. They are cultivated in pretty much the same way. Large-rooted chicory and witloof require a rich soil of fine, loose texture to a depth of twelve inches, since their roots are single, long, and round. The asparagus chicory will do well in heavier soils, since it has a cluster of shallow roots. Sow the seeds early in the spring, in shallow furrows a foot apart, and cover them lightly with fine, screened soil. When the seedlings are an inch or so long, thin them to stand an inch and a half apart. Thereafter, begin thinning when the plants are about five inches long and have a second pair of leaves. Eat the young plants thus removed and continue thinning for the table until the plants are spaced about six inches apart. When the thinning operation is completed, cut the leaves of the remaining chicory plants as often as you need them. The entire leaf cluster can be cut three inches above ground level. New leaves will sprout as often as the old are cut throughout the growing season, but the later growths, when the cool spring has given way to hot summer, are not so good as the early ones.

However, the plant grows apace in the hot summer, developing toward inflorescence. In regions where the growing season extends into the fall and early winter, the leaf growth of the chicory in these cool seasons is once more good for the table. Where the winters are mild, as in the South and along the Pacific coast, the plant remains in a static, semi-dormant state and will proceed to inflorescence in the spring. In other latitudes, such as New England and the northern states, the plant will die late in the fall and resurge in the spring from the long taproot, following the pattern of the wild chicory. The new spring growth is especially succulent and tender.

These observations apply to the three varieties named. Asparagus chicory and witloof have certain virtues that we must now note. The latter is cultivated in Belgium in a certain way and sold in the United States as the very expensive Belgian (or French) endive. It differs from other varieties of chicory in that the rosette of large tongue-like leaves tends to grow in a tight cluster at the center and form a blanched core like the heart of a celery. This tendency of the plant may be encouraged and exploited in this way: When the plant is full grown, late in the summer and early in the fall, bring all the leaves together and tie them in a bundle. Bank some soil around the plant and trim off the tip end of the leaves. In two or three weeks the center leaves will form a tight, blanched core very much like Belgian endive. The commercial producers of this delicacy dig the plant up when it is mature. They trim away the root tip, the small side roots, and the upper half of the leaves. The plants are then stored in a cool place, covered with sand or sawdust, and kept moist. In four or five weeks the endive shoot is formed and ready for the table.

Of all the varieties I have tasted, I like asparagus chicory best. Its leaves are like those of the wild chicory, and they have a very appetizing flavor eaten cooked or raw, and taken when young. As the plant develops it sends forth many shoots that resemble asparagus spears; that must be the reason why the variety is called asparagus chicory. A salad made of the young leaves and the tips of the young shoots is an incomparable treat.

ENDIVE. This superb salad green, *Cichorium endiva,* is closely related to chicory and very much like it in flavor and texture. There are two types: one has long, narrow, much-curled leaves; the other, with broad, fleshy leaves slightly curled at the edges, is named Broad Leaved Batavian, and in some quarters it is called escarole. In both types, as the plant grows toward maturity the center leaves tend to cluster tightly like those of the witloof. The more healthy the plant, the bigger and tighter will be the center cluster. The process is actually a form of self-blanching, for the clustered leaves, partially excluded from the light, will be a cream-white and pale yellow. One may promote further blanching by grouping the outer leaves and tying them together at the top.

Endive is at once cold-hardy and tolerant of heat. In the extreme South it can be better grown in the early winter; in the North, except in the extreme northern latitudes, it can be grown in the spring, summer, and early fall. It will endure a light frost, but a severe one will damage it badly. Thus, in New England and all along the northern border, October would be the terminal month for the survival of endive. All along the coastal regions, East, West, and South, one may have endive from the garden as late as Christmas. However, where one has a choice of seasons, one had better grow it in the fall. Like celery and Savoy cabbage, chicory progresses more certainly toward perfection in the declining sun of the fall than in the increasing sun of spring. Endive is tolerant of heat in the sense that the young plants, set out in mid-July and well irrigated, will grow well in the sun; but when they are full grown, they require cool, nippy weather to mellow for the table.

The sowing and cultivation procedure for endive is the same as for lettuce. For the early crop, germinate the seeds in seed flats and have the little plants ready to set out as soon as the land can be worked in the spring. For the fall crop, the seeds can be sown directly in the ground toward the end of May; and the young plants will be ready for transplanting in July. A full-grown endive plant will have a diameter of twelve or more inches; accordingly, the plants should be spaced somewhat more than a foot apart.

The ideal time to harvest endive is when the plant has nearly attained its maximum size and just before the outermost leaves begin to droop and wither and lose color. The plant at that stage will have a nice balance of green outer and blanched inner leaves. One such plant will fill the family's salad bowl to the brim.

ॐ

I come now to a group of six vegetables that are highly recommended as greens. They are inexpensive, easy to grow, and will do well in every region. They do not have an exalted status among herbaceous edibles. In a land of plenty such as ours, and because they can be grown so easily, too many people think of them as food for the poor or as animal fodder. They need to be considered more wisely. In any random aggregation of vegetables they will rank highest in food value. The body needs the vitamins and minerals they provide in abundance, and when prepared with the proper condiments, the cultivated palate will relish these vegetables at the table. Consider this fact, for example: a cup of cooked turnip greens, and these are fairly representative of the entire group, has approximately the same amount of protein and iron, ten times as much calcium, more than ten times as much vitamin A, and four times as much vitamin C as a cup of either green peas or green beans. Are you not awed and impressed? A man who feeds regularly on such greens will have the virility of a billy goat and the vitality of a stallion!

TURNIP GREENS. Turnips will grow in any fairly good soil, in one season or another, anywhere in the United States. They are a cold-hardy vegetable. That means that they will not grow with any vigor during the summer, and in regions where the summers are excessively hot they will not grow at all. The seed will germinate; the little plants will rise and try to grow; but the oppressive heat, the heat that makes the pepper and the tomato exult in life, will dwarf them. Thus the turnip is a spring and fall vegetable. It may also be grown in the winter in regions, such as the South, where winters are merely cool. Elsewhere, the best season for the turnip is the spring, and the next best is the late fall in regions where the severe frosts do not come until late November, for the turnip responds joyously to the cool fall weather and its mild, early frosts.

Turnip seed germinates rapidly, and in two and a half months from sowing the turnip will be large enough for the table. One packet of seeds is enough for a sixty-foot row. Keeping these facts in mind, sow half the packet as early in the spring as possible, and sow the other half three weeks later. For the fall harvest, get the seed in the ground late in July, and do another sowing a month later. In regions such as New England and the northern states, turnips not harvested by the end of November will be destroyed by severely cold weather. In regions where the temperature does not drop below 20° F., the turnip will survive the winter and proceed to complete its life cycle the following spring.

Grow the turnips in a neat row. Trace a shallow furrow, drop the seed in it, and barely cover it with screened or well-raked soil. In putting down the tiny seed, remember that the full-grown turnip is about the size of a baseball. The mature plants should be two or three inches apart. Therefore, work with patience and care to avoid dropping too many of the little seeds to the linear foot. Begin thinning the plants when they are several inches long and have four well-defined leaves. The plants thus removed will be ready for the table. The root will be of no consequence, but the greens will be excellent.

It is really for the virtue that is in the leaves, the so-called greens, rather than for the good that is in the root itself, that I am urging the cultivation of turnips. Or perhaps I should put it this way: for the virtue that is in the root and the greens brought together in the same pot. Yes, that's better. Greens and roots together make a very fine dish.

Turnip greens

And the time to take them both from the garden is when the leaves are a clean green, about three fourths their normal size—say six to eight inches long—and erect in posture. The root will then be about the size of a lemon. When the leaves get stemmy, lose their clean, green color, and arch backward away from the center, they have passed their prime. At that time the plant's energy will begin to go into the forming of the flowering stem, and the root itself will become progressively less juicy and more woody.

Turnip plants that are not harvested in their prime will not be a total loss. The flowering stem, when it first rises from the core of the root and is about six inches long, is a tender, pulpy, succulent shoot with a tight seed pod at its tip. Among connoisseurs of turnips, such shoots are known as turnip broccoli. Cooked and served as you would asparagus spears, they are actually the cream of the turnip crop. In my own garden I sow a late crop of turnips and leave them through the winter so that I may gather and enjoy the flowering shoots early the following spring. The venture is something of a gamble, for the winter may be too harsh for even the cold-hardy turnip to survive. Some winters, except for the plants I took in thinning the row, I've lost the entire crop. And no moaning at the bar! We who gamble to satisfy a passion have learned to accept defeat with grace.

M U S T A R D   G R E E N S .   Mustard is a leaf vegetable closely related to the turnip. In full bloom, the two plants look very much alike. Mustard greens are more pungent than turnip greens. Their mineral and vitamin content is about the same.

Mustard is cultivated in much the same way as the turnip. It is cold-hardy and will do well in any fairly good soil. Thus, it is primarily a spring and fall vegetable. Germination is rapid, and the plant attains table maturity in less than two months. A packet of seeds is enough for several twenty-foot rows.

Beginning early in the spring, sow the seeds at intervals of two or three weeks. Sow them rather more thickly than turnip seeds and begin thinning the plants when they are about six inches long and in full leaf. For the fall harvest, begin successive sowings in September. Mustard leaves are curled and frilled and broad at the top. Their color is dark green. They withstand heat better than the turnip, but they are less desirable for the table when they are full grown and the color around the edges begins to turn a reddish brown.

Watch the plants closely and harvest them before degeneracy sets in. The two most commonly used varieties are
Green Wave and Southern Curled.

Mustard greens

KALE. No vegetable is hardier than kale. Like the common dandelion, it has a passion for growth and will take
both heat and cold in stride. Thus, so far as cultivation is
concerned, it is a vegetable for all seasons and all regions.
So long as it has water, no amount of heat will do it harm,

and it will survive any winter where the temperature does not dip too far below 15° F. When it survives the winter, it will bear tender, edible leaves the following spring, and as the season progresses it will produce very desirable shoots like those of the turnip.

This, however, must be remembered about kale: although it thrives equally in hot weather and cold, it is best for the table when its passion for growth has been a little sobered by frosty weather. Its response to heat is in terms of leaf dryness and toughness; it responds to chilly weather with all the tender succulence in its nature. Accordingly, those of us who prefer tenderness to toughness will plant kale in midsummer for use in the late fall and early winter.

Kale grows on a tough, short, woody stem. Its cultivation, space, and soil requirements are the same as those for Savoy cabbage. Sow the seeds in May in soil treated as for cabbage, and transplant the seedlings when they are six inches long and have a well-developed second set of leaves. Set the plants two feet apart in rows two and a half feet apart. The two recommended varieties are Dwarf Siberian and Scotch Blue. When full grown, the plants are about a foot and a half high and have a leaf spread of approximately two feet.

The plant is distinguished by a continuous production of leaves on the upper third of the stem until it goes into the inflorescent stage. The tenderest leaves are the uppermost, near the center of the rosette. As these develop and proliferate, the ones on the lower part of the producing stem degenerate and fall off. Thus, in harvesting kale for the table, take the lower leaves that are still in good condition and leave the upper ones to grow further toward maturity. You may, of course, cut the entire plant. That has its virtue, since you will then have all the tender inner leaves. But it is needless waste and extravagance. It is more prudent to take a few prime leaves from each plant as the occasion

Kale

requires, and leave the plants to produce further until they have completed their life cycle.

The leaves of kale are thickly curled; the color is a dense, bluish green. One packet of seeds will maintain two large families in full vigor for a year!

COLLARDS. Collard greens could just as well be another name for kale, for the two differ only in unimportant ways. The collard plant is somewhat larger both in spread and height. The leaves are smooth, large, and light green. They tend to form a head like cabbage but never quite succeed. The rosette of leaves may be bunched and tied when the plant is full grown to tenderize and blanch the inner core.

For the rest, all that has been said of kale can be repeated for collards. And since repetition is tedious, we shall avoid it. We must add, however, that Georgia collards are highly esteemed in the South, and it is high time that an appropriate appreciation of this excellent and highly nutritious vegetable should spread to the North. Be it so resolved, here and now!

Collards

CHARD. This vegetable, known in some quarters as Swiss chard, derives from the sugar beet. It was developed for the edible leaves and stalks rather than for the root, which is rather stumpy and prongy, as if it were actually an abortive sugar beet. The leaves are a glossy green and look somewhat like those of the beet. The difference is that they are larger and borne on the upper end of white, fleshy stalks that are slightly curved and may be as much as two and a half inches wide. As the plant attains its full height, which

Swiss chard

is a little better than eighteen inches, the stalks tend to grow in a tight upright cluster, giving the lower part of the plant somewhat the appearance of a full-grown celery. The taste of the leaf and its texture are reminiscent of spinach—an excellent recommendation for the plant to those who enjoy spinach but are not acquainted with chard.

The plant is cold-hardy and tolerates heat as readily as kale and collards. It also produces a continuous supply of leaves, which you may cut as the occasion requires throughout the season. Take the better outer leaves from each plant and leave the inner ones to grow further; or cut all the leaves, clean and neat, about four inches above the ground. The plant will respond to either operation with new growth. Such being the nature of the plant, you can sow a single row in the early spring, take what leaves you need from time to time, and thus exploit the plants until they are destroyed by harsh winter weather. Like kale, chard is improved by frosty weather, and it will survive a winter where the temperature does not drop below 20° F. There is an alternate procedure, recommended to those who have plenty of space. The leaves of the chard are prime for the table when the plant is ten to twelve inches high. At that stage of development, or even somewhat sooner, take up the entire plant, root and all, for the table. As the plant continues from that stage toward maturity, much of its energy goes into the development of the lower stalk. Thus neglected, the leaf portion stands pat, so to speak, and loses some of its succulence. You can have prime chard throughout the season by doing successive sowings, in short rows, beginning early in the spring and continuing at three- or four-week intervals until two months before the first killing frost in the fall. In regions such as the South and along the Pacific coast, where winter temperatures are not likely to drop below 20° F., one may leave some plants of the final planting for use in the winter and early the following spring.

In sowing chard seeds, keep in mind that what are sold as chard seeds are actually little crinkled pods, each of which contains several seeds. Drop one pod every inch along a shallow furrow, cover with half an inch of screened soil, and firm it down with the foot. Water as necessary; remove weeds as they appear; and begin thinning when the plants are two inches long. At the first thinning, remove as many seedlings as necessary to provide about an inch between plants. Do the next thinning when the plants are six inches long and have a second set of well-defined leaves. Plants thus removed will be mature enough for the table. Continue thinning until the plants are spaced six inches apart.

One final word about the mature stalks, white, fleshy, and broad. Cut in convenient segments, blanched in boiling water, dipped in a light batter, and fried slowly to a soft brown in a little oil or butter, they are simply delicious. Eat them hot, crisp, with salt and pepper and a few drops of lemon juice. You may prefer them to the leafy end. If so, cultivate your chard for the mature stalks rather than for the prime leaves. Or why not for both?

CHINESE CABBAGE. This leaf vegetable may be cabbage to the Chinese, but in flavor it is more akin to mustard and turnip greens than to western cabbage. There are two types: one grows into a compact, cylindrical head a foot long and eight inches in diameter, with broad stalks and leafy ends folded over the top, variously called Chihili, Michili, and Wong Bok. The other is loose-leaved, a cluster of eight or ten white stalks compact at the bottom and flaring out in green, spoon-shaped leaves at the top. It is known as Crispy Choy. Both may be cooked as a green vegetable or used as an ingredient in soups. The first may be eaten raw as a salad. Of the two, the loose-leaved is the more desirable as a cooked leaf vegetable.

Leaf vegetables, including all varieties of lettuce, occasionally tend to bolt prematurely. As soon as the plant attains table maturity, it proceeds immediately to inflorescence and the gardener is deprived of his harvest; for, as I have noted elsewhere, when the flower-bearing stem develops, the leaves of the spinach, the lettuce, or whatever, lose their attractive-

Chinese cabbage

ness for the table. The reason for a plant's anxiety to be done with it and complete its life cycle is not clear. Those who abide by sacred folkways insist that the plants bolt because the seed was sown when the moon was waning. If there is merit in the claim, it has failed to convince me. I have never sown by the moon, and in twenty-five years of gardening I have never had a major crop failure due to bolting. Now and then some plants of a given vegetable

*Chinese cabbage—
crispy choy*

have bolted. And if some, why not all? Why was the moon so partial? Last season three chicory plants bolted, and one of a dozen cardoons went to seed. But the loss wasn't worth noting.

Premature bolting occurs now and then and that's that. The defect—or virtue—must be in the seed. If too many plants in one seeding go to seed, one simply sows again—with perhaps an eye on the moon! I mention the matter here because Chinese cabbage, more than any other leaf vegetable, though as cold-hardy as chard, tends to bolt if the seed is sown in the spring. This is a warning given by the seed grower, and one must heed it. Therefore, Chinese cabbage is a cold-hardy plant that must be cultivated for fall harvest in the North and for winter harvest in the South.

The loose-leaved variety attains table maturity in about two months; the other requires three months. Accordingly, in the northern states the seed should be sown two and three months respectively before the onset of the first severe frost. When the plant is full grown, the early frosts of the fall will tend to improve it. In the South, the seed may be sown in October. In cultivating and harvesting Chinese cabbage, the procedure is the same as for chard.

When you do your first thinning of the plants mature enough for the table, have a kettle of chicken broth ready. Add to it some mushrooms lightly cooked in butter, a bit of diced carrot, and plenty of coarsely chopped Chinese cabbage still vibrant with life. At the last minute add a beaten egg. Don't overcook. You may, however, overeat.

And with this word of caution I conclude a food-lover's garden book. What remains—some suggestions on how to prepare for the table what the garden produces—I shall present in the Epilogue. But first, a word of encouragement to anyone who has the space, the time, and the will to garden more ambitiously than I have prescribed.

I have not considered the cultivation of fruits and berries, beyond a reference to some of these that I grow in my own garden, and I have omitted a few vegetables, such as ground cherry, Jerusalem artichoke, celeriac, and poke. Nor have I considered the various melons that can be grown in certain regions of America. These omissions, however, are not due to my indifference to these good things; I am aware of their merit. But in writing my little book I chose to be selective rather than encyclopedic, and the selection necessarily reflects my personal passions and prejudices. Hence the limits within which I have worked.

And by way of encouraging such others as are not limited in both time and space and who may have different tastes, let me say this: anyone who reads these pages with care, and practices with diligence what he reads, may grow with complete success any fruit or vegetable that will thrive in the region in which he lives. The art and science acquired in successfully growing potatoes and lettuce can be applied with equal success in growing Jerusalem artichokes and corn salad. So let him expand and experiment as he wills. His seed dealer and nurseryman will tell him when and how to plant corn salad and gooseberries. The rest he knows.

The Complete Enjoyment
of Herbaceous Edibles

In that first and only perfect Garden, where every season was the ideal growing season,

> *They sat them down; and, after no more toil*
> *Of their sweet gardening labor than sufficed*
> *To recommend cool Zephyr, and make ease*
> *More easy, wholesome thirst and appetite*
> *More grateful, to their supper fruits they fell . . .*

Adam and Eve, having done sweet gardening labor, and worked no more than was necessary to make them enjoy rest and give edge to their appetite, sat to the feast and ate the fruit of their joint labors. You are now Adam and Eve. Your garden work is done. Yours may not be the perfect garden, but in the way of terrestrial gardens it is a very good one. You have a wide variety of vegetables and the necessary herbs. What remains is to use them wisely and imaginatively in the kitchen, so that you can crown your efforts with a distinguished and sophisticated cuisine. May I relate some of the ways I have used the produce of my own garden and so start you on your way?

I shall begin with a few generalizations and then spell out a number of recipes. The complete gardener who is gardening primarily to add to the enjoyment of his dinner hour ought to know certain vegetables intimately, in the raw, without the refinement of the pandering pot. Let him eat peas, carrots, celery, turnips, lettuce, artichokes—I shan't name them all—with the warmth of the sun still in them and the taste of the earth all through them; eat them there in the open garden, as I have seen my friend Mike, the pea expert, do! He would pause in his garden work, stick the shovel in the ground, mop his brow, pull up a carrot, wipe off the dirt with his hands, and eat the carrot. Or as I have seen Angelamaria, from whom I have learned much about peppers, add zest to her sales talk by snapping in two and eating the green beans she was selling at the farmer's market. Such is the mode of authentic, dedicated gardeners, a way of affirming that all is well between themselves and their herbaceous progeny.

And it is more than that. Such communing with vegetables in the raw serves a very useful purpose: their taste and texture live in the memory, and with such intimate knowledge of them, one will deal more wisely with them in the kitchen. Granted all that may be claimed for eating them raw, we normally eat our peas and carrots cooked. And every vegetable that is not properly cooked is a shameful desecration of nature. This needs to be driven home without mercy, for it is in the kitchen that some of the finest vegetables too often come to a miserable end. And who better than the gardener himself, who has grown it and knows its taste and texture in the raw, can tell when his spinach has been ruined in the kitchen?

Let us proceed to the kitchen, then, where we shall earn

our crown of leeks by mastering the fundamentals of vegetable cookery. And I suggest that we put ourselves in the proper frame of mind by listening to the creed of the strict vegetarian; not for what he denies, which is the merit of meat, but for what he affirms, the virtue of vegetables. His zeal may properly lead us to a sober reappraisal of vegetables in the diet and in good eating. We cannot eschew meat and eat only vegetables, but as gardeners we must affirm that vegetables should be eaten in greater quantities than they are at present in the ordinary American home. And they will be eaten more abundantly and with more relish when the cook learns to prepare them with taste and imagination.

How can this be done? We begin with the premise that vegetables should be absolutely fresh. And they are, since as gardeners we bring them directly from the garden to the kitchen. Now they must be properly cooked. Rule number one: don't overcook them. Don't bring to the table a dish of spinach cooked to death and dripping with water. There may be a dietary objection to overcooking vegetables in water: nutritionists warn us that when vegetables are cooked too long in water the soluble nutrients are sent down the drain, unless one drinks the water. The water being generally unpleasant, it is seldom drunk, and the drained vegetable is devoid of its best food value. Well, I confess that I have no idea what percentage of its total nutrients is lost when spinach, for example, is overcooked in water. Nor do I care in the least. My objection to over-cooking is purely aesthetic: what is lost is flavor and texture. And not infrequently, the two are one. Can one easily distinguish between the flavor and the crisp, crack-ling succulence of celery? It may well be that the crackle, the succulence, and the flavor are one!

How can we know when a vegetable is cooked just

enough? The answer cannot be precise. It cannot be expressed in the number of minutes that the vegetable should be left on the fire; nor can we put into precise words the appearance of a properly cooked vegetable, its response to the fork, the feel of it in the mouth. We can approximate an objective description and that's about all. We learn by experience in the kitchen checked against our knowledge of vegetables, and that is why I have stressed the importance of knowing certain vegetables in the raw. He who knows a prime raw carrot, and knows it well and appreciates it, will have no difficulty knowing when that carrot is properly cooked and distinguishing it from one that is overcooked. Test yourself in this way. Take a piece of a prime carrot and cook it to death; take another and cook it just to the point where it still has some slight, faintly crunchy resistance to the bite; check the two against a third piece of the same carrot uncooked. Do the same with green beans, peas, and other vegetables. Then draw whatever conclusions you may!

As we deepen our intimacy with vegetables, we gardeners learn that they differ in the fineness and fragility of their texture and that some are more susceptible than others to the ruin of too much fire. All vegetables in their absolute prime for the table are more tender, more fragile, than those that have begun to stiffen and toughen with age. That's pat! However, *some* vegetables in their absolute prime are more fragile and tender than *others*. Knowing in which category a given vegetable belongs, we can proceed more wisely with it in the kitchen. Prime asparagus, peas, spinach, zucchini, for example, are more fragile than prime cabbage, kale, broccoli, and collards. Therefore, it takes less time to ruin the first group. Root vegetables, too, differ in the degree of their sensitivity to fire. A potato baking in the oven needs less surveillance than a turnip boiling on the stove, and a beet will survive more fire than a carrot. These things we learn by experience.

If I were asked how to tell when a given vegetable is sufficiently cooked, and how to avoid overcooking it, I would answer that there are two tests, visual and tactile. The experienced eye can see with considerable accuracy when a vegetable is sufficiently cooked. "Ho ho, the beans are done," says the astute cook, having uncovered the kettle and peered at the beans. Whereupon he picks one up from the kettle, feels it with the fingers, bites into it, and—sure enough— it is done. Or, the same cook, having been detained on the phone or otherwise distracted, runs to the kitchen, peers at the beans, and says, "Damn it! The beans are overcooked." And, sure enough, the tactile confirms the visual test.

Now, what did the astute cook see? What did he feel that confirmed what he had seen? I have already confessed the difficulty, if not the impossibility, of describing with *precision* the appearance of a properly cooked vegetable. We can say, however, that the astute cook actually saw the proper degree of edible tenderness. When the green beans were dropped into the boiling water they were round and firm and the pods were tightly closed. He who knows a prime green bean can actually see its firmness, the drum-tight nature of its surface. When the bean is cooked just enough, the pod begins to loosen at the seam where the two halves come together; the surface texture is visibly more loose; the roundness, or compactness, if the bean is not of the round pod variety, is somewhat less pronounced. Having seen these characteristics, the astute cook proceeded to feel and to taste; but he did so in complete confidence that these tests were a mere formality. Or he may try a bean with the prongs of the fork and note that it is easily pierced with a little pressure. He holds it horizontally athwart the prongs and notes that it bends slightly. The taste, of course, is always the final arbiter. When he bites into the bean, the cook will note, as I said above of the carrot, some slight, faintly crunchy resistance to the pressure of the teeth and will detect in it a trace of the flavor of the raw green bean.

When in the second instance the cook cursed his negligence and said that the beans were overcooked, he had seen that these characteristics of the properly cooked bean were too far advanced and that the bean had entered the stage that would lead to disintegration: the pod was partly open, the texture was too loose, the compactness was disappearing. And the cook knew that when it was given the final test, the bean would be found to be as pap to the taste.

I have used the green bean as an example, but the generalization applies as well to other vegetables. Leaf vegetables dropped in boiling water quickly proceed from the proper degree of cooking to an undesirable disintegration of the leaf tissue. Note the virility, firmness, the herbaceous life that are in a leaf of freshly washed raw spinach. The astute cook strives to retain some degree of these characteristics in the cooked leaf. The properly cooked leaf shall have lost its firmness, of course, but it will be intact and recognizable as a leaf of spinach and will still have some of its original texture. The overcooked leaf, disintegrated, fallen apart, shall have lost its identity and texture altogether. At its worst, it is an amorphous, mushy, watery mess.

To avoid such desecration of vegetables by overcooking, one must proceed with rigorous care in the kitchen. The heat of our stoves, electric or gas, is deadly when turned on full power; therefore, the more fragile the vegetable, the more exacting must be one's surveillance while it is cooking. It is never wise to put any tender vegetable, such as fresh peas, green beans, spinach, asparagus, on the heat and then leave the kitchen for whatever reason. Too often one is distracted and fails to return in time to remove the vegetable from the fire at the moment when it is cooked just enough. Nor is it ever wise to start a vegetable cooking, turn off the heat when it is about done, and then leave it on the burner on the assumption that what heat remains will be just enough to cook the vegetable just right. In most instances the heat that remains will be just enough to overcook the peas, the spinach, or whatever. As a matter of fact, it is not even wise to remove a vegetable from the fire when it is nearly done and leave it in the pot, for even off the fire the vegetable will continue to cook for several minutes in the heat that remains in the water. The conclusion is obvious: stand by while the vegetable is cooking; look at it and test it frequently. When it is done, remove it from the fire and from the pot in which it was cooked.

Another method of cooking vegetables is by braising. This means cooking a vegetable directly in butter, oil, bacon fat, a combination of these, or even in a light sauce, with the possible addition of just a bit of water or other liquid. For example, peas can be braised in this way: Put as much butter or oil as you like in a saucepan. For peas for four people, mince a green onion and two green leaves of lettuce. Sauté these gently in the fat. Add the fresh peas, salt and pepper to taste, stir well, cover the pan, and simmer over a slow fire until the peas are cooked. No liquid needs to be added. There is enough in the fat and in the ingredients themselves; but the pan must be well covered to prevent its escape by evaporation.

Which is the better method? It is a matter on which I refuse to take sides. Braised peas will taste somewhat different from peas cooked in salted water. Which do you prefer? There is merit in both; the important thing, I must repeat, is to avoid overcooking. So why not vary your ways and use both methods?

In our kitchen we use both methods and often combine the two. I enjoy now and then fresh green beans cooked just right in salted water, with no condiment whatever, but I enjoy them even more braised in olive oil with a bit of minced ham, a touch of tomato sauce, a few minced leaves of fresh basil, salt, pepper, and a squeeze of lemon juice. So I have them, the one way or the other, as desire urges.

In general, however, whether I use the one or the other method depends on whether the vegetable is very young or somewhat past its prime. Nearly all vegetables can be braised when they are young and juicy, but they had better be boiled when they are older. Boiling in salted water both tenderizes the vegetable and eliminates some of the bitterness that is the consequence of age, especially in all leaf and root vegetables.

It is frequently said against boiling that both flavor and nutrients of vegetables are lost in the water; this is doubly true when a vegetable is overcooked. I avoid such loss by combining braising with boiling. When I proceed in this way, however, the boiling is brief: the vegetable is blanched rather than cooked. The cooking is then completed by braising. Let me give you an example. We had spinach the other evening prepared in this way: When the leaves were washed, I cut them coarsely in order to manage them more easily in the pot, and plunged them into boiling salted water. They were mixed thoroughly in the boiling water and kept in it, with the lid on, for no more than two minutes. They were then taken immediately from the fire, drained, and pressed gently with the hands to rid them of nearly all the moisture. Then I minced them thoroughly with a chef's knife. There were still life and texture in the spinach, visible to the eye and perceptible to the touch. I put in a skillet three tablespoons of olive oil and a small pat of butter, into which I minced very fine a large clove of garlic. When the garlic was barely browned over a gentle fire, I put in the minced spinach, added pepper and the juice of half a lemon, and mixed the whole thoroughly so that spinach and seasonings were nicely assimilated. A gentle simmering in the covered skillet for two minutes and the spinach was ready to serve. It was not in the least watery; the texture was just right; and the condiment gave it a pleasant taste. A generous serving of the spinach, a nicely grilled steak, a couple of slices of good bread, half a bottle of wine, and the dinner was well-nigh perfect!

This procedure, with such variations as one's taste and the particular vegetable may require, is recommended for all greens and most other vegetables. There is a reason for every detail in the process. The preliminary blanching in well-salted water is a way of cooking the salt evenly into the vegetable; it reduces the bulk of the vegetable so that it can be easily managed in the skillet where the cooking will be completed; and it boils away some of the harshness and bitterness from the less delicate vegetables such as mustard and turnip greens, collards, and cabbage. The thorough mixing and slow simmering in the skillet effect an even distribution of the seasonings.

The time required for the blanching process is determined in each case by the vegetable itself and by its general condition when it is brought from the garden to the kitchen. Spinach, since its leaves are very fragile, will always require less time than other leaf vegetables; and when they are immature, the leaves will require less time than when they have attained maturity. And all of them when they are very young, as when they are taken up in the thinning process, may require little or no blanching at all. We have often minced such young tender greens and braised them directly in the cooking fat without blanching.

The seasonings, of course, will always reflect the taste

and resourcefulness of the cook. Here one may suggest but never dictate. A condiment that we have always found most satisfactory is the meat juices of roasts and pan-fried steaks and chops. When, for example, we cook pork chops in the skillet, we remove these when they are done and finish cooking the turnip greens in the fat left in the pan. We skim off some of the fat if there is too much of it, or we may skim it all off and replace it with a touch of olive oil and butter. Or we may enrich the meat juice by adding seasonings such as garlic, shallots, parsley, lemon juice, tomato, Tabasco.

The time required for preparing the cooking liquid and simmering the vegetable in it is never very long, so roasts, steaks, and chops can be kept warm in a low oven without in any way impairing their quality. However, if one is using the meat juice of pan-fried steaks or chops, he can keep the meat warm by laying it lightly over the simmering vegetable—lightly so that the meat will not be saturated with the taste of the vegetable. Roasts, because of their weight and bulk, cannot be kept warm in this way. Well covered with foil, they will rest nicely in a warm oven until it is time to serve them.

Naturally, the value of meat drippings used as a condiment will be enhanced if they issue from properly seasoned chops, steaks, or roasts. A chicken taken from its wrapping and put in the oven to roast will leave in the roasting pan little else than melted chicken fat. The same bird, stripped of its gobs of fat, laved with olive oil tempered with a bit of lemon juice or wine vinegar, with bits of sage, celery, parsley, garlic, and onion put in its cavity, and the whole carcass sprinkled with salt and pepper, will leave juices so fragrant that one's stomach will churn with yearning. But I must urge no further, for, as I said, in these matters we may suggest but never dictate.

The less delicate, more substantial greens—the firm-tissued collards, kale, mustard, turnip, Savoy cabbage—so rich in food value and so good when properly prepared, are rather strong in grassiness and require a richer condiment than does spinach; their strong, wild sort of taste must be balanced with a correspondingly strong but more familiar taste in the condiment. I suggest this rather simple, leanish sauce. For the amount of greens an ordinary family would consume at dinner, mince to a pulp about two ounces of lean salt pork. Cut it into thin slices and then with a light cleaver or heavy chef's knife pound it with the cutting edge until it is reduced to a paste. As it spreads out under your blows on the cutting board, keep folding it in and pounding until the job is properly done. It will take a few minutes. When thus reduced to a paste, put it in a skillet with two tablespoons of olive oil and a touch of butter. Now mince very fine three shallots or onions, two cloves of garlic, and the leaf tips of a stalk of celery. Add these to the salt pork and sauté over a slow fire. Do not burn or unduly brown—which you are certain to do unless you control the heat. Add next a third of a cup of tomato sauce, an equal amount of beef or chicken broth, and the juice of half a lemon. If you like a suggestion of piquancy in your sauce, add two or three drops of Tabasco or a small chili pepper. Simmer the sauce for a few minutes, then add the blanched, well-minced greens. Mix thoroughly, cover the skillet, and complete the cooking.

I have given you the recipe in detail not so much to dictate as to suggest the kind of condiment that these not-too-familiar greens require. Follow it to the letter or vary it to suit your culinary whims. This sauce is also recommended as one in which the more mature green beans, cardoon stalks, and the larger artichokes may be cooked after they are blanched. The stalks of cardoons are prepared for blanching in precisely the same way as celery. To prepare an artichoke for cooking, remove the small, lower bracts and cut about an inch off the tip end. Trim the rest cutting away the tough outer green portion until you get to where the bracts are bleached and tender. What remains may be somewhat loosely called the heart; loosely because it will be considerably larger than what is sold commercially as an artichoke heart. Cut it in quarters, remove the choke, and the trimmed artichoke is ready for blanching. When cardoons and artichokes are cooked in the sauce here suggested, a handful of grated Parmesan cheese mixed with a few bread crumbs may be added during the last few minutes of simmering. Are you with me? The crown of leeks is within your grasp!

And now a final word. No matter how carefully a gardener sows according to his family's requirements and how faithfully he consumes the fruit of his labor so as to avoid waste, it is not likely that he will be able to eat the entire harvest of a vegetable when it comes to maturity. What then? How shall he cope with the surplus? Root vegetables that cannot be otherwise stored can be left in the ground for a considerable time beyond the stage of maturity that renders them prime for the table. Their quality will be somewhat impaired, but they will still be edible. Peas, green beans, peppers, asparagus, the entire cabbage group, and all the vegetables listed in Chapter 9 except endive and garden rocket, he may cook and freeze. Shell beans can be shelled directly into a container and frozen without cooking or blanching. They are the only vegetable known to me that can be dealt with in this way without the slightest impairment to their texture or taste, even if they are left in the freezer a year or more. Trust your guide, for he would not deceive you!

As for the rest, everyone will have his favorite freezing

formula. Blanching, cooling, freezing are the normal procedure. We have found that the best results are attained if the vegetable is frozen after it has been completely cooked and ready to serve with the appropriate condiment. For example, cook your greens as suggested in this chapter, put them in containers in whatever quantity is adequate for a family meal, cool them, and tuck them away in the freezer. You will be pleased with the results.

We'll now round out this discussion of fundamentals in vegetable cookery with a few specific recipes, especially ones that illustrate the use of herbs. Again the intent is to suggest, not dictate; in fact, the hope is that you will want to vary my suggestions.

In writing about herbs in Chapter 4 I promised that I would tell how they can be used in cooking chicken; let me tell you first how to prepare a chicken for the oven, be it a fryer or a roaster. Sprinkle the cavity with salt and pepper. Put in it two cloves of garlic crushed, four or five leaves of fresh sage, two or three sprigs of parsley, half a small onion, a few leaves of celery. Lave the whole chicken with olive oil and the juice of half a lemon. Salt and pepper it well. Tuck leaves of sage and sprigs of parsley between the body and its wings and legs. Let it set overnight and then roast it in any way you please.

Or proceed in this way: Dust a cut-up frying chicken with flour. Brown the pieces on both sides in olive oil, using a large skillet with a lid. When done, add to the skillet a teaspoon of minced tarragon, a teaspoon of minced parsley, and two minced cloves of garlic. Salt and pepper to taste. Mix thoroughly the chicken and the herbs, and cook for a few minutes over a slow fire. Then add half a glass of dry white wine. Increase the heat, shake the pan vigorously; when the wine is reduced by half, cover the skillet and finish cooking the chicken.

Vary the recipe by using rosemary in place of tarragon. Vary it again by using parsley and thyme. Vary it further by using only shallots and parsley. Determine for yourself the proper amount of each herb. And always avoid browning and burning the herbs. That ruins their flavor.

For a savory combination of chicken and artichokes proceed as follows: Dust with flour and brown the chicken pieces in olive oil or whatever fat you like. Season with salt, pepper, a crushed clove of garlic, and half a glass of wine. While the chicken is cooking over a slow fire, braise four pared and quartered young artichokes in olive oil, crushed garlic, parsley, salt, pepper, and the juice of one lemon. When these are nearly done, combine them with the chicken and finish cooking the two together.

In preparing a four-pound cut of pork for roasting, proceed in this way: Make incisions in it three inches apart, of varying depth, and about an inch wide. Press to the bottom of each incision a leaf of sage and half a clove of garlic. Sprinkle salt and pepper in each incision. Salt and pepper the entire surface of the roast, and it is ready for the oven. The reason for varying the depth of the incisions is to secure an even distribution of the seasonings. When possible, it is better to flavor the meat a day before it is roasted. While it is roasting, baste it frequently with white wine. Do roasts of veal and lamb in the same way, and vary the use of herbs as you please. Prepare roasts of beef in the same way, but use only garlic, salt, and pepper, and red wine for basting.

We have, thus far, better than twenty recipes for cooking meat and fowl; and these are but suggestions to get you started on your way. Here are two more, which may prove to be even more richly suggestive. One is for cooking nearly all kinds of fish. Let us begin with three pounds of sole.

Mince four shallots, one clove of garlic, four large sprigs of parsley, a dozen salted capers, and a dozen leaves of English pennyroyal, *Mentha pulegium,* and sauté in half a stick of butter. Stir in a bit of flour for thickening. Add a cup of dry vermouth and the juice of one lemon. If you need more liquid, use beef or chicken broth. Add salt and pepper to taste. If you want piquancy, add a dash of Tabasco. Simmer the whole slowly for ten minutes, then put through a blender. Enrich with a third of a cup of light cream. The sauce is done.

Dust the sole with flour and brown lightly in olive oil. Pour the sauce over them, turn up the heat, and when the sauce begins to bubble briskly, cover the skillet, shake it well, and turn off the heat. Let it rest for five or ten minutes while you sip a very good martini. Then eat it. And having eaten it, ponder the ways in which you may vary the theme, remembering the resources of your garden.

Here is a lamb stew. Remove as much of the fat as possible from a three-pound boneless shoulder of lamb and cut it into bite-size pieces. Dust them with flour and brown them lightly in a small quantity of olive oil. Remove the meat and put in a baking dish. Skim away most of the fat from the skillet, and add a dab of butter to the meat juice that remains. Sauté lightly in it, over a slow fire, the following, minced very fine: six shallots, a clove of garlic, the leaf ends of two stalks of celery, a small carrot, and six sprigs of parsley. When these are nicely cooked, add a cup of dry white wine and simmer until the liquid is reduced by half. Now add a cup of beef stock with a teaspoon of flour dissolved in it, the juice of half a lemon, a dash of Tabasco, and a quarter cup of tomato sauce. Simmer the whole for a few minutes, salt and pepper to taste, and pour it over the meat in the baking dish. Mix in it a tablespoon of rosemary leaves chopped very coarsely and cover the dish. Finish cooking in a 350-degree oven for about forty-five minutes.

A variation of the spaghetti sauce given in Chapter 6 can be made by substituting two tablespoons of minced, lean salt pork for the steak. A more simple sauce for pasta can be made by adding plain tomato sauce to parsley and garlic sautéed in olive oil or butter. You can readily devise other sauces if you keep in mind your stock of herbs and how they may be used.

I shall now tell you how to make minestrone, a famous soup that only the complete gardener can make as it ought to be made. Note how it reaches into the resources of your herb and vegetable garden. In prescribing the quantities I shall be thinking of substantial servings for eight.

In a large soup kettle, six- or eight-quart capacity, boil in two quarts of water, one quart of fresh-shelled romani beans, taken either from the vine or the freezer. When thoroughly cooked, cream the beans by passing them through a food mill and then combine them with the water in which they were boiled. This will be your thick bean broth.

Using a chef's knife or a sharp cleaver, mince to a paste a quarter pound of lean salt pork. Add to the paste six large shallots, the leaf tips of one stalk of celery, two cloves of garlic, six sprigs of parsley, and the leaves of one sprig of thyme, all chopped fine. Sauté all these ingredients in two tablespoons of olive oil over a slow fire, using the kettle in which the soup is to be made. Do not brown or burn. Add two large, peeled ripe tomatoes. Lacking these, use canned tomatoes or four ounces of plain tomato sauce and a cup of beef broth. Simmer the whole in the covered kettle for fifteen or twenty minutes. This is the sauce, the important flavoring agent for minestrone. It must be thickly fluid, so use whatever amount of beef stock is necessary. Sprinkle generously with black pepper.

Dice one medium carrot, one medium potato, and four stalks of celery, and braise in the sauce. While these vegetables are simmering in the sauce, chop coarsely half a large Savoy cabbage, two large leaves of chard, several bud ends of the zucchini vine, and one medium zucchini. Add these, stir the whole thoroughly, cover the kettle, and braise gently for ten minutes. The braising cooks the flavor into the vegetables. Now add the bean broth and as much beef stock as necessary to produce a thick but fluid soup. Bring to a boil, taste for salt, reduce the heat, and simmer gently for half an hour. A few minutes before serving the soup, stir in half a cup of finely minced basil.

Such is the classic minestrone. If you like rice or pasta, in it, cook whichever you like separately, a third of a cup per person when cooked, drain, and add to the soup at the same time as the basil. Instead of the pasta or rice one may prefer the soup ladled over a slice of toasted French bread lightly rubbed with garlic. The final touch is a generous sprinkling of grated Parmesan cheese.

Quick-frozen minestrone can be kept for as long as a year without deterioration in quality. Therefore, make large quantities of it and freeze it when herbs and vegetables are flourishing in the garden. Or one may simply freeze the vegetables braised as directed, and have them on hand. The bean broth can be made as needed. Lacking fresh-shelled romani beans, a can of black bean soup is not a bad substitute. Or one may omit the bean broth and make an excellent soup by adding the desired amount of beef or chicken stock to the braised vegetables. Work out your own variations; you have a rich and substantial theme.

The finest beef or chicken broth, or the two combined, you can make in your own kitchen by using the resources of your garden. For the two combined, proceed as follows: In a gallon of water put three or four pounds of chicken backs and necks, or a small stewing chicken; add two large, meaty, beef soup bones, or an ox tail, or three pounds of lean beef short ribs. Add salt and a dozen peppercorns. Bring to a boil, then reduce the heat and simmer slowly until the meat is nearly done. Flavor the broth with a stalk of celery, a leaf of chard, a small carrot, half an onion, six large sprigs of parsley, and one ripe tomato or a cup of tomato juice. Continue the gentle simmering for half an hour, and the broth is done. Strain, skim off the fat, and serve in small bowls—it's so good and so rich!—with croutons and grated cheese.

Now one final recipe, and you are on your own. This one is for that lovely vegetable-and-egg dish called *frittata*. The name is Italian. There is no English equivalent. Literally, it means a fry, but since it is always a fry of something the name of the principal ingredient is usually specified. For example, a spinach *frittata*. The procedure in making it is always the same. Here is the way to make it with spinach: Blanch, drain, and mince enough spinach to yield a cup per person. Finish cooking it in a skillet, using enough oil or butter to grease generously the bottom of the pan. When the spinach is done, distribute it evenly in the skillet, pressing it down gently with the fork. The skillet should be of such size that the level spread of spinach is about an inch thick. Shake the skillet several times to make sure that it does not stick. Beat two eggs per cup of spinach, stir in salt and pepper, and pour over the spinach. By spreading with a fork and shaking the skillet, achieve an even distribution of the beaten egg; it is the binding agent. Cook over a gentle fire for about three minutes, or until the egg at the bottom of the skillet is well set; then finish cooking under a preheated broiler, the pan about six inches away from the heat. When nicely browned on the surface, the *frittata* is done. Loosen with a spatula, slide it onto a serving tray, cut it as you would a pie, and serve it confidently. An alternate way of cooking it is to put it in an oven preheated to 500 degrees after the egg has been added to the spinach.

The variations on this theme are numerous. A *frittata* may be made with leeks or green onions, using *all* of the green leaves that are sound, and some cooked potato finely diced. It can be made with chard or young mustard greens, or hearts of artichokes cut in fine pieces. One of the best is made with diced zucchini and zucchini blossoms with the bitter stamen removed. Or use any combination of these vegetables you desire.

The beaten egg can be flavored with minced chives, parsley, chervil, basil, thyme, tarragon, or several of these combined. Or add some grated cheese to the egg, a heaping teaspoon for every two eggs. To the vegetable base you can add thin slices of pork sausage cooked separately, or sausage meat, cooked and well shredded. And for a final touch: Line the skillet with paper-thin slices of salami or prosciutto; spread the cooked vegetable on top. Pour on the beaten egg. Work it in evenly by shaking the skillet and probing with the fork. Cover the surface with slices of salami or prosciutto. Press them gently into the egg but keep them on the surface. Proceed with cooking as directed.

The vegetable base for *frittata,* completely cooked with all condiments, can be frozen. Prepare and store as much as you like while herbs and vegetables are flourishing in the garden, but remember to freeze it in several containers, each with a measured number of servings in it. Then, when the snow drifts and the wind howls, you can sip a martini, beat a few eggs, and enjoy a *frittata* of zucchini and zucchini blossoms. A touch of summer in one's cozy kitchen in the depth of bleak winter. *Buon appetito!*

Mail-Order Sources

SEEDS AND POTTED HERBS

Earl May Nursery
Shenandoah, Iowa 51601

Henry Field Co.
Shenandoah, Iowa 51601

Tool Shed Herb Nursery
Salem Center
North Salem, N.Y. 10560

Wayside Gardens
Mentor, Ohio 44060

Weston Nurseries
East Main St.
Hopkinton, Mass, 01748

White Flower Farm
Litchfield, Conn. 06759

SHALLOTS

GNL Shallot Distributors
51 De Shibe Terrace
Vineland, N.J. 08360

Les Eschalotes
Ramsey, N.J. 07446

Index

A

acidity, soil: *see* PH factor of soil
Agricultural Extension Service
   stations, test soil samples, 23
alfalfa, 167
alkalinity, soil: *see* PH factor of
   soil
anise (*Pimpinella anisum*), 72
annual herbs and vegetables, 40,
   70, 73, 96, 125
aphis, 138, 161, 210
artichokes, globe (*Cynara scolymus*), 10, 11, 38, 40, 54, 82, 127,
   200–5, *illus. 201;* sauce for, and
   cooking of (recipe), 245–6
arugula: *see* rocket, garden
asparagus, 4, 40, 130–3; trench
   for, 130–1, *illus. 131;* cooking,
   238, 239
asparagus chicory: *see* chicory,
   Italian dandelion or asparagus

B

basil, sweet (*Ocimum basilicum*),
   72, 85, 104–8, *illus. 107;* uses
   for, 106–8; preserving with parmesan (recipe), 108–9
bay: laurel (*Laurus nobilis*), 9,
   59, 60, 85; California (*Umbellularia californica*), 59–60
beaked parsley: *see* chervil
beans, 167–76; green or snap, 8,
   35, 49, 52–3, 167–8, 169, 171,
   174, 192; pole, 36, 37, 40, 168,
   169–71, *illus. 170, illus. 172;*
   green-shell, 53, 168, 169, 171,
   175–6; wax, 168; bush, 168,
   169, 171, 174–5; lima, 168, 171;
   soybeans, 168, 171; fava, 167,
   168; cooking green, 238, 239,
   240; braised green (recipe),
   242; sauce for mature green
   (recipe), 245

A Note About the Author

Angelo Pellegrini was born in Casabianca, Italy, in 1904, and came to this country when he was ten years old. He grew up in McCleary, Washington, and attended public schools there. As a young man he worked as a section hand, lumberjack, court interpreter, and longshoreman. He graduated from the University of Washington, where he received his Ph.D. in English literature, and has taught English there since 1930. He and his family make their home in Seattle.

Dr. Pellegrini's first book, *The Unprejudiced Palate,* was published in 1948, and was followed by *Immigrant's Return* in 1951, *Americans by Choice* in 1956, and *Wine and the Good Life* in 1965. He has been the holder of a Guggenheim Fellowship, and in 1951 was given the Freedoms Foundation award for significant contribution to an understanding of the American Way of Life. For some time his column, "Notes on Enjoyment of Bread and Wine," appeared in the Seattle *Post-Intelligencer,* and the Seattle *Times* in the past year has been running his series "Native Land Revisited."

A Note on the Type

This book was set on the Linotype in GRANJON, a type named in
compliment to Robert Granjon, typecutter and printer—in
Antwerp, Lyons, Rome, Paris—active from 1523 to 1590.
Granjon, the boldest and most original designer of his time, was
one of the first to practice the trade of type founder apart from
that of printer.

Linotype GRANJON was designed by George W. Jones, who based
his drawings on a face used by Claude Garamond (1510-1561)
in his beautiful French books. Granjon more closely resembles
Garamond's own type than do any of the various modern faces
that bear his name.